Ronan and Erwan Bouroullec

H.L.

Phaidon Press Limited
Regent's Wharf
All Saints Street
London N1 9PA

Phaidon Press Inc.
180 Varick Street
New York, NY 10014

www.phaidon.com

First Published 2003
© 2003 Phaidon Press Limited

ISBN 07148 4318 0

A CIP catalogue of this book is
available from the British Library

Texts by Ronan and Erwan
Bouroullec, David Toppani,
Claude Aïello, Giulio Cappellini,
translated from French and
Italian by Shaun Whiteside

Design: Geoffery Cottenceau
and Julien Gaillardot in collaboration with Ronan and Erwan
Bouroullec
Printed in Hong Kong

Thanks to everyone who has supported us for the past thirty years

Ronan and Erwan BOUROULLEC

CONTENTS

1
IN THE BEGINNING

The year is 2003. We are thirty-two and twenty-seven years old.

It's hard to locate the starting point for our work. One beginning might be these two people: Giulio Cappellini and David Toppani, and these three projects: the « Lit Clos », the « Disintegrated Kitchen » and the « Hole » collection; they form a starting point both for our work and for this book.

Ronan started working on his own when he left school. A succession of projects and exhibitions took him through to 1997, when he launched an exhibition at Neotu Gallery and showed his kitchen at the Salon du Meuble in Paris. David Toppani made the prototype.

Erwan produced some pictures and the technical plans. He was the first person to work with Ronan. He was still a student, and was approaching the business of design step-by-step. He was doing an assistant's job on Ronan's drawings. Concurrently, Erwan was designing the « Lit Clos ».

Sure, we're brothers. We have a similar underlying culture, but we haven't experienced the same things at the same time. We're quite different, and we've had to learn to work together, at the same table. It's a permanent dialogue, striving towards a common goal, and you don't get there without a fight.

Giulio Cappellini met Ronan when he saw the kitchen. For about twenty years his company has delivered unique products, unique procedures: radical choices, daring, courage. The structure is typically Italian; far from any kind of large-scale industrialization, it's based on a network of small subcontractors. The region where he's based is like a beehive, the cradle of all the big Italian brands.

It all started there: on the one hand there was the Italian flexibility that gave us a lot of leeway

← Erwan Bouroullec,
painting, oil on canvas
1997
Ronan Bouroullec,
first projects from
1995 to 1997

in developing our projects, and on the other there was Giulio's keen, demanding and protective eye. The kitchen was the starting point, after which we brought out the « Hole » collection and the « Lit Clos », amongst others.

The « Disintegrated Kitchen » and the « Hole » collection contrast with, or partially complement, one another. The kitchen presents a new typology in terms of a particular market. It simply suggests breaking away from both the idea of the made-to-measure and the integrated. Conceived as a piece of furniture, it is based on an idea of flexibility: building simply, far away from the wall, like a table that you put down and then take with you when you move. The « Hole » collection was more traditional, in terms of its simpler typologies: shelves, a console, a table.

The « Lit Clos » is based on a similar principle to that of the kitchen. It works on an unfamiliar scale, closer to architecture, but also employing the logic of furniture, as an element that is autonomous in relation to the more general infrastructure of the house.

David Toppani was the first to make prototypes of our projects. David is well removed from the industrial style of production, he formalizes our drawings according to an adept logic that helps to give shape to an idea: that is the germination of a future project.

Giulio Cappellini led us to our first industrial reality: open, daring, communicative. Confident in the choices he makes, he took us a long way, to a place where profit is more complex than a best-seller.

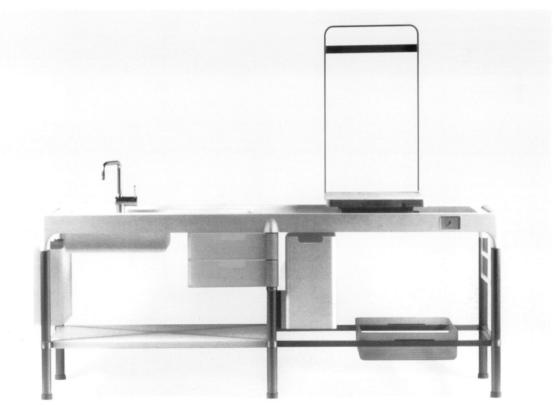

1
« Disintegrated Kitchen »
1998
Cappellini, Italy

1

2

The Lit Clos

The « Lit Clos » puts forward a simple idea. It's a box that's sufficiently closed to accommodate a bed and the intimacy that it presupposes, and at the same time sufficiently open not to be claustrophobic. The box is on an architectural scale, between a bed and a bedroom.

It uses techniques from furniture manufacture: painted plywood, soldered steel, and above all there's the DIY assembly of the kind that you get with a piece of Ikea furniture. These characteristics give you a certain ease of assembly and of installation. While it's admittedly more complex than an ordinary bed, it's still simpler than putting a bedroom together. There is a play on the scale of the space. The « Lit Clos » frees you from the necessity of building a whole bedroom, and opens up numerous possibilities in relation to the place where one sleeps.

The « Lit Clos » exists in a low and a high version, respectively 70 cm and 180 cm off the ground.

70 cm

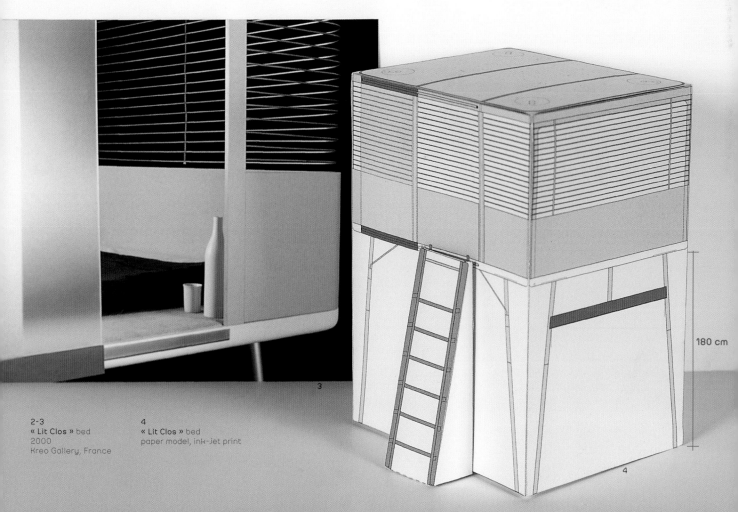

180 cm

2-3
« Lit Clos » bed
2000
Kreo Gallery, France

4
« Lit Clos » bed
paper model, ink-jet print

3

4

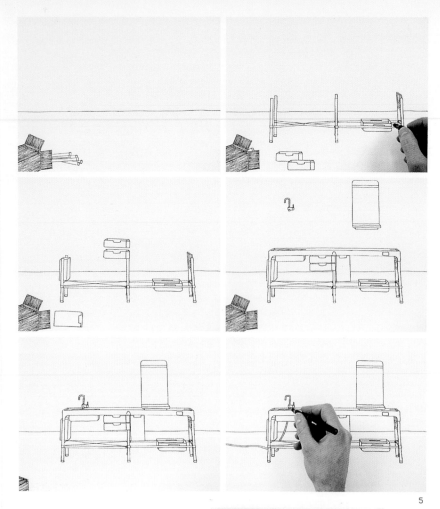

5

5
« Disintegrated Kitchen »
extract from the DVD
A Motion Notebook by
Fulguro, 2002
Edition Kreo-Bouroullec

6
« Disintegrated Kitchen »
photomontage

6

I met Ronan Bouroullec in January 1998, at the Salon du Meuble in Paris, where he was showing his design for the « Disintegrated Kitchen » in the VIA exhibition. I was immediately fascinated. Over the past few years I've found it increasingly difficult to find designs that thrill me from the minute I see them, but in that particular case the « Disintegrated Kitchen » struck me with the lightness and poetry of its language. I immediately wanted to meet its creator, and I met Ronan.

Ronan Bouroullec is exactly like his designs: light, discreet, ironic, professional. From that moment a splendid collaboration of studies, research, designs, prototypes and products began. Shortly afterwards Erwan started working with his brother, and our dialogue became even more interesting, because Ronan and Erwan complement one another in terms of their single identities. Working with them is always a great pleasure and a great learning experience.

The constant quest for the greatest possible expressivity in a project, without taking anything for granted, and a profound desire for self-criticism are at the root of their great mastery and uniqueness within the current panorama of contemporary design, in which everything is often too simple, too familiar, too much taken for granted.

All the designs that we have produced with the Bouroullec brothers, and those that we are working on at present, arouse my enthusiasm because each time we open a new chapter in our collaboration, a new chapter in the bond between us, we realize that it's only by working hard that you can arrive at really good products.

After that first kitchen, in 1999 we created the « Hole » collection of tables and consoles, made in curved wood with a crystal and wooden top. This was followed in 2000 by the « Hole Chair » constructed entirely out of varnished aluminium, characterized by a smoky chrome effect rendered by a skilled craftsman who normally varnishes Harley Davidson motorcycles.

These two designs signed by Ronan were followed in 2000 by the « Spring Chair », designed by Erwan, which is enjoying increasing success in the market. This product combines the elegance of slender contours with great comfort, thanks to an adjustable head rest not unlike those used in cars, and a foot rest with a special mechanism that adjusts itself according to the person's weight. In 2001 we presented the « Glide » sofa, designed by both brothers, as a natural evolution of the « Spring Chair ». In 2003 the sofa was awarded the prize for best piece of upholstered furniture by the international jury of *Elle Décoration*. In 2001 they presented the « Brick » bookshelf system, one of the pieces that best expresses the design poetry of the Bouroullec brothers.

In the same year, we made the « Console with Mirror » and the « Console with Bowl and Vase » in a co-branding operation with Corian® Designs that, although originally produced for a show, ended up being part of the Cappellini catalogue.

The following year we presented the « Samouraï » armchair, the fruit of precise research into the use of new materials such as expanded polyurethane foam which, covered with a fabric, forms the structure of the back and the seat. In 2003 we showcased the « Butterfly » shelves, conceived the previous year, which have a resolutely architectural presence.

All their designs are now co-signed by both brothers and, beginning with the polystyrene « Clouds » that were originally made for an installation and that will soon go into production, we're working on new designs intended to represent a defiance of boundaries, halfway between art and technology.

At my age I've learned two very important things in my dealings with Ronan and Erwan Bouroullec: the humility and the pleasure of working, and above all the desire to keep on telling people of new dreams: dreams that the Bouroullec brothers turn into objects for everyday use, to help people pass their time as agreeably as possible.

Phaidon: Can you describe your activity?

David Toppani: When I started out, I was basically making architectural maquettes. Then I turned towards the production of models of industrial objects, prototypes as well as limited series for galleries. We also do a lot of work with designers: often via agents, associations or institutions. I'm thinking particularly of the Kreo Gallery, which is one of our main clients. Finally, we work on behalf of industrial firms, who also need designers. We intervene at the point when the three-dimensional maquette is being realized. We've made prototypes for Tefal, Seb and Absolut, for example. It's a matter of producing maquettes, fake objects that can be used to validate the form and the technical principles.

P: What's specific about your work for designers?

DT: When you're working with designers, the whole commercial side is discussed with the agent. On the other hand we deal directly with designers on everything relating to the object, because they conceived it and follow its 'birth'.
At the beginning, they send us documents: plans, drawings or study models. On the basis of these elements we start production. We regularly meet with the designers and make study maquettes to refine the project. Then come the last finishing touches: choice of colour, appearance and marking of the product. We use all kinds of material: wood, plastics, resins, finish paint, furniture paint. It depends on the project; on the « Honda Vase », for example, at the request of Ronan and Erwan, we used bodywork paint. And that's how the vase got its name: it corresponds to a Honda colour reference.

P: How did you meet Ronan and Erwan Bouroullec?

DT: I met Ronan first, around 1994-5. He'd been asked to come up with a perpetual office calendar for the Paris Mint. He needed a maquette and I made it. He'd just come out of the École Nationale des Arts Décoratifs; he was very young. Since then I've worked on lots of Ronan and Erwan's projects: the « Parasol Lumineux », the « Disintegrated Kitchen », the « Combinatory Vases », the « Coffee Cup n 4 », the « Lit Clos », the « Audiolab », the « Polystyrene House » for the Noailles villa, a single-flower vase and various other objects. While initially we only have to produce a single

example, the order may go far beyond the scope of the prototype. For example, we have realised the « Vase » for Kreo Gallery in eight pieces, plus an additional two artists' proofs. In the end, we're the ones who produce them all. The most interesting part is shaping the object, that means realizing the first edition. I don't like making the copies so much: it's less interesting, and contrary to what you might think, it isn't necessarily any faster, because they're all hand-crafted. We've produced all the pieces for the « Honda Vase », the « Vase » and the « Lit Clos ». But unless there's an industrial process factored in, everything's hand-crafted.

P: How would you describe your collaboration with the Bouroullecs?

DT: Ronan and Erwan have a pared-down formal vocabulary, and a precise idea of where they're headed. They know the exact proportions that they wish to give to their objects. They're very demanding about details, about the quality of the work, and generally fairly precise about the choice of colours: they provide a reference, and then they come to check it. If they realize that the result isn't in keeping with what they'd originally imagined, we adjust it. They know what they want and what they don't. They're not hesitant, or at least not too much. The completed project very closely resembles the original design: they don't tend to call their original intention into doubt.
As far as we're concerned the hardest thing is to gauge the time you're going to devote to a project, with the Bouroullecs just as with our other clients. But from a human point of view it's very enriching to work with them. There are people I have good professional relations with, but it stops there. With the Bouroullecs it goes a lot further.

7	8	9
« Hole Shelf »	« Hole Console »	« Hole Table »
1999	1999	1999
Cappellini, Italy	Cappellini, Italy	Cappellini, Italy

2
MULTIPLES

We've never designed a unique piece, or at least we've never thought of an object in those terms. Multiplying, mass-producing, is *a priori* the basis of our work. For us an object is always destined to be abandoned, in the context of a system of distribution that means that the piece slips away from us. The object is designed, perfected, then sold: the system is fairly chaotic, and its rules can be surprising.

In art, generally speaking, a work is autonomous. But with an ordinary object, once it's out of the factory, it has to seduce within a context that is no longer within the designer's control. And besides, mass production in a global market is a complex terrain. By virtue of being reproduced and distributed on a worldwide scale the object imposes itself, through its very distribution, in an authoritarian manner. You have to understand that for an injection press that produces a plastic chair in a few tenths of a second, the expensive thing is stopping the machine.

The « Combinatory Vases » are based on a double game: producing, in eight moulds, a set of pieces that have no function in isolation; combining those pieces to assemble a vase, the number of configurations is almost infinite. It's a way of producing a certain diversity in series, to try to escape authoritarianism, to hand the job over to the user.

Habits of sugar consumption vary considerably from one country to another. The foreign distributors who were interested in « Coffee Cup n 4 » collided with this reality: the space reserved in the saucer to present the sugar corresponds to a format that is principally used in France.

The bottles made for Issey Miyake are the most proliferous objects that we've designed. The cosmetic sector is the most industrial environment we've encountered so far.

10
« Combinatory Vases »
1998
Cappellini, Italy

11

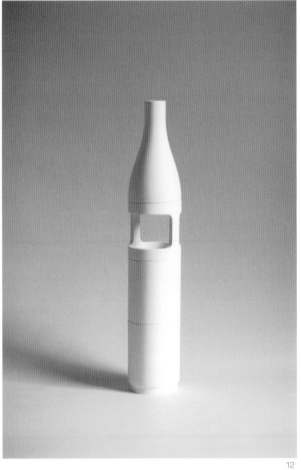

12

11-13
« Combinatory Vases »
1998
Cappellini, Italy

13

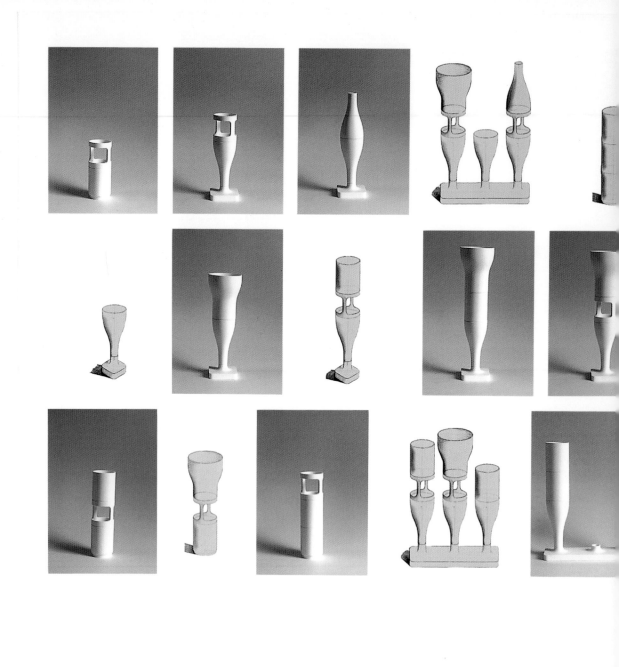
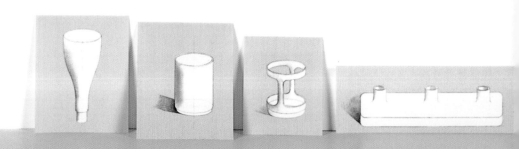

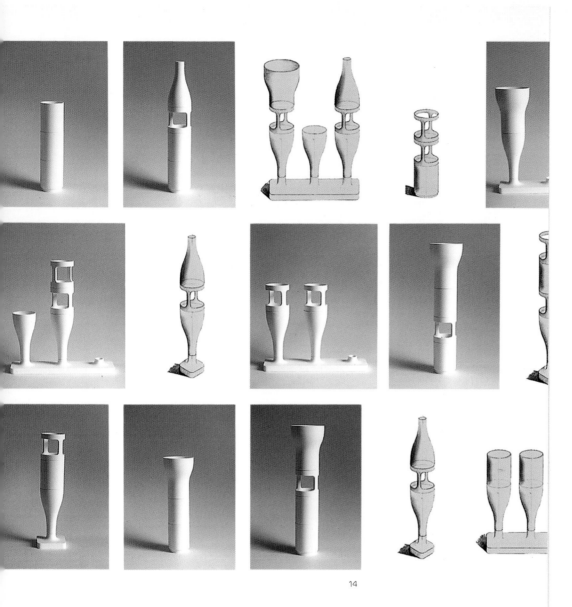

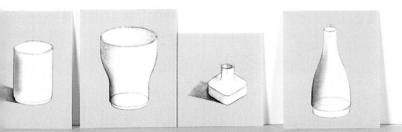

14
« Combinatory Vases »
1998
Cappellini, Italy

15
« Combinatory Vases »
drawings

17

16

18

16
« L'Eau d'Issey »
range of scented body
products, packaging,
2002
BPI for Issey Miyake,
France

17
« L'Eau d'Issey »
range of scented body
products, packaging,
models

18
« Coffee Cup n 4 »
1998
unrealized project

3
FIVE SEATS

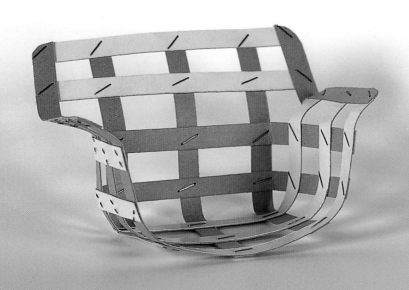

The seat is perhaps the object to which people are most attentive, particularly because the body gives its own advice. As far as we're concerned, it's one of the typologies that demands the most precision from us. Everything about it is very tense: forms, materials and thicknesses echo one another in a jumble of comfort-solidity-look, in which a thickness, an angle and a curve intimately interlock in a kind of house of cards.

The « Outdoor » armchair for Ligne Roset folds away, and can be used outside. Everything is based on a principle of sewing and hinges which, when you unfold it, forces the seat and the back into a curvaceous shape, and when folded back again lets them revert naturally to the state of sheets. The seat and the back are cut from sheets of plastic that are then inserted into the sewn part, a bit like the visor of a baseball cap. The base is articulated so that it can be folded. Here, comfort is based on the torsion of the sheets that fold beneath the body's weight. A sense of reassurance and safety is derived from the fabric, a technical material intended for sport, hyper-resistant to everything. This sheet-based construction isn't without its problems: its thinness and absence of volume don't match up to the typical idea that people have of comfort.

The « Safe Rest » is a daybed that also exists in double depth. Here the principle is very simple. The structure is made of two arched tubes that form the outline. These tubes are connected by perpendicular crosspieces. The whole is covered with a fabric that folds underneath the couch, where it is strapped and stretched like a corset. This cover is a sewn sandwich, composed of

canvas on the underside, foam, and wool blanket on the topside. The seams, parallel lines five centimetres apart, have a structural role.

The « Spring Chair » is the first seat we designed for Cappellini. Its manufacture is quite traditional in Italian industry: a shell covered with foam, then with fabric. What guided us here was the idea of a system: add two elements, make four different typologies from them. Comfort was of prime importance. The foot-rest is articulated on a spring that responds to the movement of the legs. The head-rest is adjustable, as is found in cars.

The « Hole Chair » was also designed for Cappellini. First, the aluminium sheets are cut out by laser, then stamped and folded. This laser cutting produces two-dimensional elements that are the flat versions of the feet, the seat and the back. At the level of the seat, the stamping creates a slight hollow, and for the back it creates a protruding lip over the rim of the window. The folding lifts the back, and also serves to shape the feet. Each fold and stamp is structural, reinforcing, line by line, what started out simply as a featureless metal sheet. Finally the seat is soldered and painted.

The « Samouraï » armchair applies the idea of disassembly that occurs in suits of armour. Each piece addresses a part of the body of the seat. But, quite unlike armour, each yoke (of rubber-fabric sandwich) has its own flexibility.

19

19
« Outdoor » armchair
2001
Ligne Roset, France

20
« Outdoor » armchair
0.5 scale model

21
« Outdoor » armchair
0.2 scale model

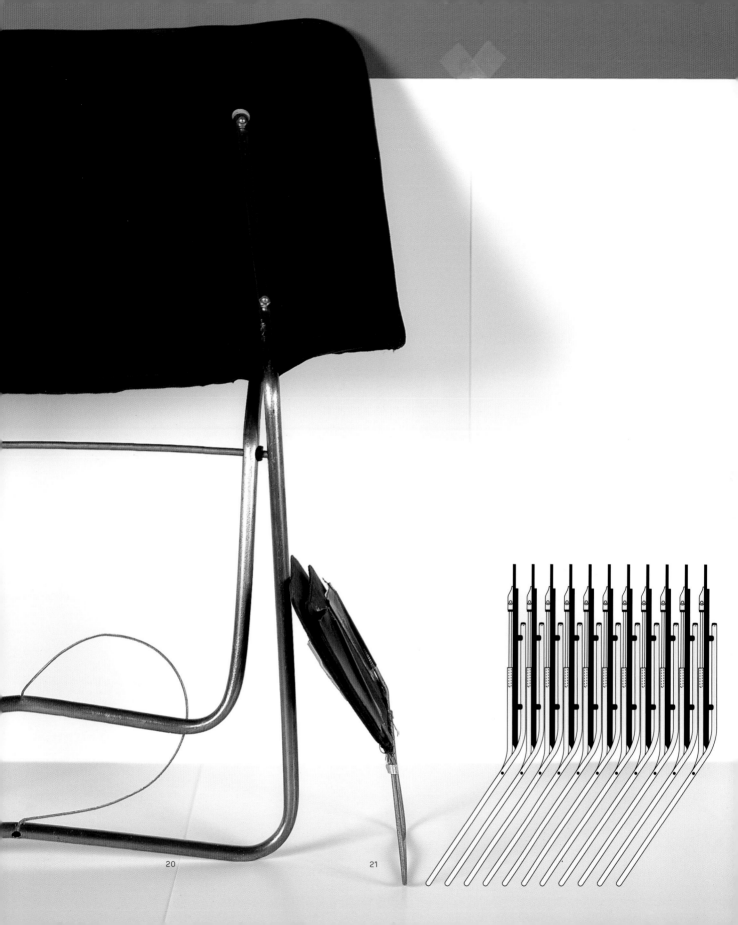

23

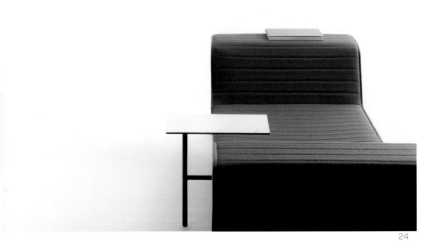

24

22
« Safe Rest (large) »
daybed
1999
Domeau & Pérès, France

23-24
« Safe Rest »
daybed
1999
Domeau & Pérès, France

25
« Spring Chair »
2000
Cappellini, Italy

26
« Spring Chair »
prototype

27
« Spring Chair » detail,
head-rest

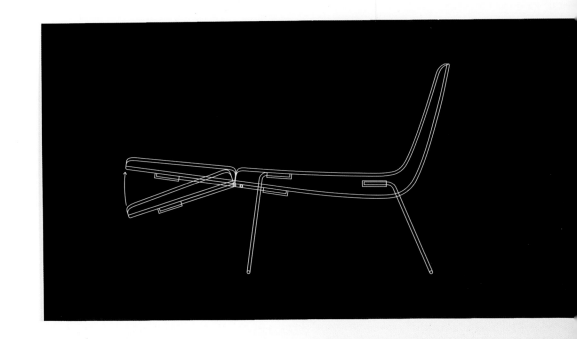

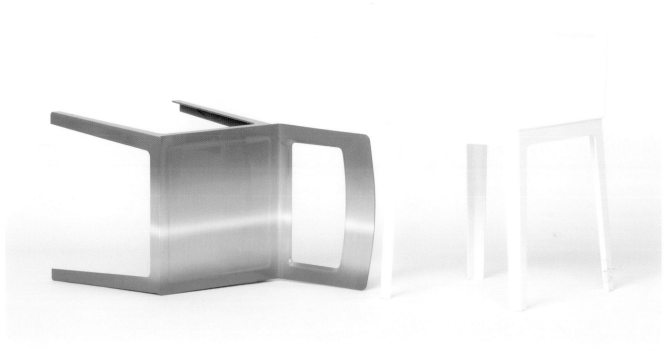

30

28-29
« Hole Chair »
details

30
« Hole Chair »
2000
Cappellini, Italy

31
« Samouraï » armchair
2002
Cappellini, Italy

32
« Samouraï » armchair,
exploded

FIVE S HTS

4
FACTORIES

We began our collaboration with Vitra in January 2001.

Initially this was mainly an ongoing discussion with Rolf Fehlbaum, the chairman of Vitra, and his technical director, Egon Brauning. Our position was a special one because we were a long way from any kind of culture linked to the office environment. Without terms and conditions, and with no themes imposed on us, we just produced drawings for a few months. These sketches covered more or less all the elements that can be found in the workspace, and others that we planned. Our apprenticeship in the office environment involved a lot of coming and going: our propositions led to further discussions, which refined our perception, and then we produced new designs, and yet more.

During the following year, numerous prototypes were substituted for the sketches. The scale tests confirmed intuitions, or revealed impasses in certain directions. Eventually we settled on the idea of the big table.

The project was originally constructed around its ambition, and subsequently around the problems it threw up. As we went about confronting this reality, the project with Vitra took shape. This process is an uncertain path in which you discover the particularities of each person and each thing; in which you learn that industrial reality is not universal. A factory is a market, a tool, a history. All of these aspects have their own characteristics, each having an impact upon the project: a good project is the successful alchemy of an encounter.

Lucia: These are your first designs for office furniture. Is it essentially different from domestic furniture?

Ronan: They are two different things and therefore present different problems. But we actually do our best work when we apply ourselves to things that we initially know little about. If you don't have any fixed ideas about a particular topic, you can approach it entirely free from preconceptions. We can do something new simply because our view is not inhibited by established patterns.

L: This design is conceived for people who want to work together. You both work together, so did your collaboration serve as a model?

R: Design requires the ability to analyze a situation and the partners with whom one is working. We find it particularly inspiring to span the gap between different disciplines. And Erwan and I also regard design very clearly as a matter of teamwork. The interesting thing about our working method is that we take up contrary positions at the outset of the design process. We often disagree and clash with one another for a considerable period of time, so that when an object leaves our workshop, it has already survived a number of battles.

Erwan: Besides, our workshop is like a two-way street; no object belongs to one person or the other. This is the primary concept that we wanted to bring into this project. We said to ourselves 'We are going to make something spacious, with generous proportions, something with larger dimensions than an object that belongs to me alone, where I store my own stuff'. The principle of working together is secondary to the principle that nothing belongs to any single individual.

L: Where did you get the idea for the table? A 'common tool' for 'communal work'?

R: The initial idea was to regard the hundred square metres of office space in which about fifteen people work as a landscape, and to provide a living setting for these people - because one also 'lives' in one's office. 'Communal work' means that approximately fifteen people live together in a room. They must be able to discuss things together; there must be proximity between colleagues but one also needs quietness in order to concentrate, as well as the opportunity to relax. In order to cover such a spectrum of diverse situations, one needs an object that unites all of these qualities. And we saw that in the table.

E: First we worked on the problem of the large open space. And then, metre by metre, we made the small decisions.

L: The table strikes me as a very old patent. Our history, our memories are populated by many tables...

E: Yes. Design often stands for new ideas. What we are doing here is not exactly a new idea; I would be more inclined to say that we have transplanted an idea. Our design actually has more in common with a large table that might be found on a farm or somewhere in the countryside. It is an image that is implanted in the memory: a large table at which someone is sitting and reading the newspaper, while someone else in front of him is peeling potatoes, and a third person at the other end is mending his watch.

R: Our grandparents lived on a farm where the kitchen table was the central focus of the house. This table was the place where people ate, where they talked, and I'm sure my father did his homework there. It was just a surface. Today you have to think about where to situate the electric hook-ups, and how to divide up the surface, because when fifteen people are sitting at a table, everyone needs a little space of their own.

L: You said that one also lives in the office. We frequently hear of the increasing intermingling of leisure time and work; in this context the question arises as to whether design is contributing to this development.

R: In our case, our private life and work are not really distinct. Our workshop is a room that must be comfortable, simply because we spend so much time there. For this reason, we have carefully examined the archetypal elements of the office, and attempted to transfer situations onto them that would normally be regarded in a domestic context. For example, the objects are covered with fabric because of its visual, textural and acoustic qualities. The next problem was to create a homogenous landscape that is also complex. Think about the fact that you might have an old sofa from your student days, and next to it, if you've acquired a little more money in the meantime, a wonderful Vitra chair, stereo equipment by Sony and, to crown it all, a wall full of old books from the flea market... The real-life diversity of such an interior landscape is very important to us. For this reason, the landscape that we have designed for Vitra consists of materials, colours and shapes that correspond to each other, but simultaneously offer marked diversity. One finds textiles here and metal there, plastic in between, small details next to large surfaces, et cetera.

L: One has the impression that you had a good time designing this diversity; in fact it is often stated that your work has something 'playful' about it. How do you view this?

R: Our office is not 'playful' in the literal sense of the word, but its flexibility gives it a certain suppleness and simplicity; it leaves room for movement. If someone was looking for an analogy, a film by Jacques Tati might be appropriate. But in spite of everything, an office is an office, not a beach or a café. An office is a living space in which people sometimes like to sit together and talk, but also need to be able to work at a high level of concentration. It is a little bit like a restaurant: in a restaurant you can celebrate, but on another occasion you might find yourself in the position of telling someone that you are going to leave them. The things that we make don't satisfy a playful impulse like fireworks do, but belong more in the category of 'tools' - tools that provide enjoyment.

E: It was important for us to create an open system. As we work, we often imagine that we are creating a palette; but the palette is reconfigured by the people who will later use it. I wouldn't call this 'playful' design, but it gives people the opportunity to adapt to the room in which they find themselves.

L: Then spaciousness is not just a question of surface area, but has something to do with freedom?

E: Yes. Sometimes people talk about creating their own landscape. Our goal is not to create a perfect work environment in which the telephone has a specific, predefined place. Some people like boxes to put everything in; others like a lot of space so that they can leave their things lying around; and others like to have everything within reach. Our job is to make all of this possible and especially not to restrict anyone with a predefined framework.

R: A life that is the epitome of organization, because some ingenious designer thought of absolutely every contingency when he was making an object, doesn't seem that appealing.

L: Are your projects designed for the present - in the sense that you take the current status of things as a starting point, see what is missing and search for new solutions? Or is it more like a vision for the future, a prescription for what might come?

E: The problem does not lie in the future. Unwritten rules prevent me from having something to eat at my desk, or from having a place near my desk where I can read a book. Our design offers the potential to support a way of life that already exists elsewhere.

R: I recently read something that Duchamp wrote a long time ago. He said, 'Things used to be better, because there were no solutions and therefore no problems.' Now there are many solutions and so we are surrounded by problems. It is often said that progress means the constant development of new solutions, applications and functions. We have taken the contrary position of reaching a point with our office design where there is a surplus of options. For example: if you have a coffee cup, the cup has a particular place; you have a vase, the vase has a place; a pencil, the pencil has a place. Everything is divided up into little squares: a different function has been created for every possible activity. Nowadays, few inventions are truly inventive. The way we see it, the definitive question posed by an office is this: 'What does one really require?' And above all: 'Can't anyone offer a partly blank page, so that when a person wants to set down the coffee cup, there is simply a place to put it? And if someone wants to have a vase, he goes out and buys a vase and puts it on the table.'

L: That gives your designs an almost magical aura of simplicity. The table is a very simple object that also distinguishes itself by what is missing - there is nothing superfluous about it - and yet one can use it in an endless variety of ways.

R: Simplicity and humour are prerequisites for the emergence of a natural whole. So that every little change that a user makes in the office, every idea that he wants to realize, is completely natural. So, when he wants to move something from one place to another, he only has to think about how to achieve this in purely physical terms, and doesn't have to ponder the social/psychological question: 'How can I explain to everybody else that I just felt like doing it?' Humour and simplicity are prerequisites for the emergence of something like friendship. I think that when people come into physical contact with this system, they will be compelled to move things around, and they won't feel inhibited. On the contrary, they'll feel as though the table is thoroughly satisfied, as though it was just waiting for something to happen.

33

37

40

34

41

44

35

38

42

45

36

39

43

46

47

48

Joyn office system
a two-year process
2002
Vitra, Switzerland

33-34, 36, 38-43, 45-46
single desk studies
15/01/2001

35
office study
21/02/2001

37
screen study
17/04/2001

44
combined desk study
21/02/2001

47-48
photographs of
maquettes
23/01/2002

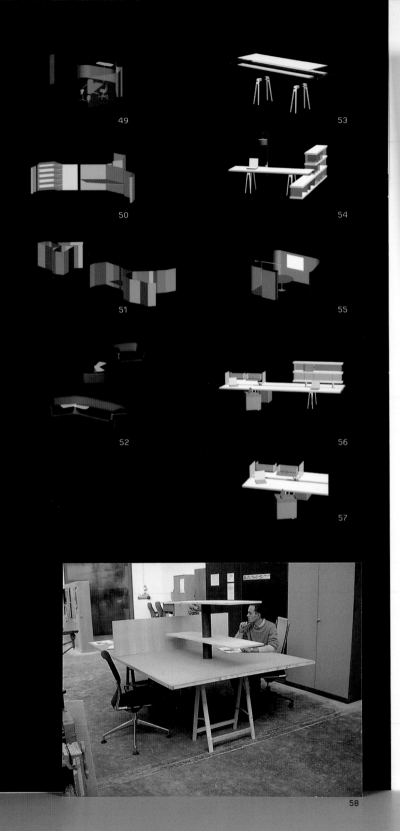

49

53

50

54

51

55

52

56

57

58

59

49-51, 55
screen studies
17/04/2001

52
desk screen study
08/03/2001

53-54, 56-57
desk studies
05/11/2001

58
Erwan working on a
prototype
12/10/2001

59
prototypes
07/02/2002

60
office study
14/01/2002

61-62
maquettes
23/01/2002

63-64
details

65
maquette
19/04/2002

66

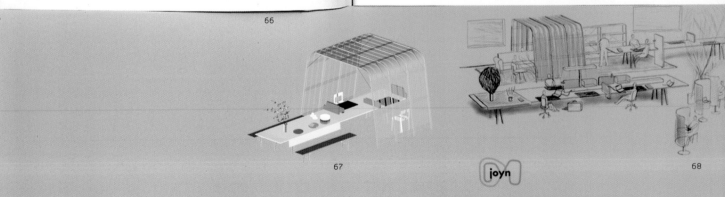

67

joyn

68

66
catalogue: *Workspirit 8*,
Vitra,
01/10/2002

67
final sketch
29/05/2002

68
final sketch
09/06/2002

ROLF FEHLBAUM
Chairman of Vitra

The design process is not a pleasure ride, but an excursion fraught with many frustrations. It is a sequence of trial and error and the danger of failing is ever present.

It is true that if you reach your goal and arrive in the promised land, you forget all the frustrations; then the pleasure of having found the right path is overwhelming. Often, however, you do not arrive, and many projects get lost on the way. As in any excursion, the chance of succeeding depends on the choice of the destination and the composition of the team.

So the most important decision I have to make for Vitra is the definition of the design project and the selection of the designer. Since there are so many good designers, it is difficult to know how to proceed; how to avoid making mistakes. And it is particularly difficult for Vitra to find new designers, given that we have worked with some of the best in the past.

Our first ever choice was decisive. In 1957 my father got a licence to produce the Herman Miller Collection in Europe, and the choice of the first designers was made: Charles and Ray Eames and George Nelson. That was before my time, but I was involved when Verner Panton came with a vacuum-formed model of something that later became the « Panton Chair ». Most of our active design relationships date back a long time: more than twenty years with Mario Bellini; almost as long with Antonio Citterio; more than ten years with Jasper Morrison, Ron Arad and Philippe Starck; while Alberto Meda and Maarten Van Severen joined in the mid-Nineties.

A new relationship that has had a major impact on Vitra started in November 2000 when I met Ronan and Erwan Bouroullec. What makes me so optimistic about the relationship? That so many of the ingredients that make great design possible seem to be present in the Bouroullecs, and that two years later we have a first result, the office system « Joyn », which I and many others find very promising.

What are these ingredients? First of all an understanding of the needs of the project and the desire to find the right solutions. Energy, dedication, curiosity and a fresh new approach to problem-solving are also essential elements. Technical understanding is of course important. An eye for future trends and the ability to conceptualize are necessary if one wants to enter new territory. The ability to integrate one's competence and experience with those of the producer usually enhances the result, provided the designer can absorb this without losing his own individuality. Enthusiasm on both sides is crucial. It often leads to a strong emotional relationship between designer and producer, which helps to overcome the frustrations that are inevitable in the process of creating something new. And of course the designer must have the ability to give form in his own characteristic way, to create visual constellations and organizations of elements that provide the viewer and user with pleasure and sometimes happiness. Finally, a factor of growing importance is a talent for communicating the ideas behind the new design.

The combination of Ronan and Erwan - two very different personalities with a lot of common ground between them - is a very fortunate one. Working together they combine so many of these ingredients. Mixing brotherly intimacy and competition they challenge each other, creating a dialogue that moves things forward: sooner or later, they have to come up with a solution that they can both accept. Some of the greatest achievements in design have been the result of such co-operations. Think of Charles and Ray Eames. And never ask which of the partners made the more important contribution, as this question ignores the very nature of this extraordinary and enormously productive collaboration.

69
« Joyn » office system
table
2002
Vitra, Switzerland

70-72
« Joyn » office system
different environmental
situations
2002
Vitra, Switzerland

73-74 →
extracts from the
presentation film for
« Joyn »

joyn is communal

joyn is communal
work...

well...

75
« Joyn » office system
detail
2002
Vitra, Switzerland

5
A WORKSHOP

We've never manufactured anything ourselves. As far as we're concerned, design is a two-handed business, in which we do the designing and someone else does the manufacturing.

Claude Aïello is a ceramicist, originally from Italy, who lives and works in Vallauris. He's a specialist in throwing pots, and his workshop is smaller than a kitchen. At the beginning of the twentieth century, Vallauris made utilitarian ceramics, which flooded the market in the South of France. As the century advanced, this ancestral technique shifted from an almost industrial level (in terms of quantity and destination) to a craft-based output. Old photographs show the streets of the village covered with plates and bowls left in the sun to speed up their drying.

There are strong similarities between sketches and the speed of pot-turning: when the drawing doesn't work you screw the piece of paper up into a ball: likewise, when the object that's just been turned on the wheel is a failure, you crumple the clay up into a ball. The drawings that we brought with us from Paris were quickly forgotten in the Vallauris studio. Thanks to Claude's fast way of working, we outlined our ideas and transferred them instantly to the wheel, in the way you would use a sketchbook. When he turns the clay, it's enough to ask him to pull or push a bit to make the shape develop.

While turning pots imposes certain rules and traditions, the techniques themselves haven't evolved much for thousands of years. Claude is so skilful that the range of possibilities is very extensive. The days spent in that studio watching the clay being turned have brought into being objects that oscillate between testimony and formal invention.

If it's important for us nowadays to work in a field that extends from industry to craft, it's because this project has made us aware of the fundamental richness in the diversity of means of production.

76

Torique Collection
1999
Gilles Peyroulet Gallery,
France,
Cultural Affairs,
Provence-Alpes-Côte
the collection as a whole
was commissioned
jointly by the Regional
Department of d'Azur,
(Ministry of Culture), and
the town of Vallauris

76
« Torique » Jugs
1999
Gilles Peyroulet Gallery,
France

77

78

77
« Torique » jug
1999
Gilles Peyroulet Gallery,
France

78
« Torique » tables
1999
Gilles Peyroulet Gallery,
France

79
« Torique » vases
1999
Gilles Peyroulet Gallery,
France

80

81

80
« Torique » oil lamp
1999
Gilles Peyroulet Gallery,
France

81
« Torique » stool
1999
Gilles Peyroulet Gallery,
France

82
« Torique » fruit bowl
1999
Gilles Peyroulet Gallery,
France

82

Cutting

On the wheel, the piece is wet, the clay is still soft. It's almost finished, round, symmetrical. Then comes the moment when a turner adds a handle or a spout, or pushes the sides to distort them.

Using a knife, Claude Aïello takes the jug, that at this stage is more of a bottle and with two cuts incises a T-shape. He separates the two lips of the T, then brings them back together to shape the spout. Finally, he uses a little water to bind them and stretch the new rim.

Once again the knife, and this time just a single vertical cut. Two trunks are divided to form two bowls, two stools. Then the pieces dry. Before they are placed in the kiln, the turner pares off any bumps and corrects the verticals. Then he fires them.

83

84

85

86

87

When I met Ronan, he was working on his own. That was right at the start, in 1999; he was just leaving school and finishing his education. The project commissioned by the town of Vallauris and the Direction Régionale des Affaires Culturelles was intended to bring a designer and a craftsman together. Ronan came to Vallauris and visited a number of studios. He was certainly attracted by the pieces that were in my studio. He asked me some questions, but he didn't say anything to me. Then the project organizer called me up to say, 'Mr Bouroullec would like to work with you.'

I'm a turner. My father, both my grandfathers and my great-grandfather were turners. Italian by origin, I arrived in Vallauris in 1964, at the age of thirteen. I'm the eldest of a family of seven children. My first school certificate was from Italy, and subsequently I went to school in France. I left six months later to take a three-year apprenticeship for my certificate as a ceramic turner. As there were a lot of children in my family, my father guided me towards a trade rather than into academic study. He was lucky that I liked it, and that I took it seriously. I served my apprenticeship with Saltamacchia, one of the biggest manufacturers in Vallauris. My father worked there as a kilnsman.

In 1974 I started up in my own right and began working to commission. Today I have clients all over the place, in France and even abroad. I also work a lot with Moustiers Sainte-Marie, a village of potters. Over the past few years I've stopped making multiples, and started specializing in single pieces.

Ronan worked with me throughout this project. He came perhaps six or seven times, during the weekend arriving on Thursday evening and staying until Sunday evening or Monday morning. We preferred weekends, when the mind is calmer. Ronan came with sketches, including the one for the « Torique » jug. He was surprised to see me turning the form he'd designed in record time; it takes a quarter-of-an-hour, half-an-hour at most to make a bottle. You go through a sequence of different shapes, you widen it, you narrow it, before reaching the desired object. He was fascinated by the malleability of the material, the ease of working with the fingers, and all that gave him other ideas. Hand-turned pottery allows you to get close to the forms of any sketch, although it does get more difficult

once you start moving away from rounded shapes.

I start by taking a mass of clay that depends on the size of the piece I want to make, turning the material with my hands until I'm getting close to the desired shape. I work with an electric wheel. Then I leave the piece to dry for twenty-four hours. Next comes the finish: I refine the base or I add it on, I make collages, I add some relief. Then I leave it to dry for between forty-eight and seventy-two hours.

After that I put the piece in the kiln that has been preheated for one or two hours to get rid of any moisture. I fire it at 1000 degrees for between five-and-a-half to six hours, all depending on the load in the kiln at the time. I leave it to cool for at least ten hours outside the kiln. After this first firing, the piece is called biscuit.

Then I apply the enamel: it's a powder that comes straight from Limoges; I dilute, mix and apply it to the piece. Once the enamel has dried I fire it again, but for a shorter time than previously: four-and-a-half to five hours at between 960 and 990 degrees. I make pieces ranging in size from an egg cup, a candlestick or a thimble up to a piece measuring eighty centimetres or a metre: it could be a dish or a vase made in a number of pieces.

The objects designed by Ronan are more pointed than most of the objects that I usually make. It will never be possible to make them in large numbers, because of their shape. The spout of the jug, for example, took a lot of work: you have to open it up like a window and then do some gluing, some modelling. It's quite pointed. We started with a placemat, a kind of fairly thick doughnut. Then Ronan had the idea to hollow a trench into the thickness of the doughnut's rim: that was the birth of the two-sided vase. Technically it's fairly complex, particularly for the big model, because you have to ensure that the two sides have the same thickness. We made a coat hook, an oil lamp, a fruit bowl, a stool, a necklace: we couldn't stop. Eventually we had to, because we were limited by the number of pieces. Otherwise the project wouldn't have been accepted. We weren't working for ourselves, but for a commission.

It was a fantastic experience. I love the purity of the lines, the forms. With my wheel I try to refine the shape, to get as close as possible to the original sketch, to apply the finishing touches. Sometimes you encounter a few technical problems, as with the double-sided vase. It was hard to get two sides of equal thickness and equal height, because the external side needed to have greater mass than the internal one. Then Ronan wanted matt and gloss enamels on the same piece, but when it came to firing it, a thermal shock was created in the kiln because the internal part of the vase was much colder than the outside, and when the temperature rose, the piece shattered. It took me a few months to solve the problem. But in the end the vases are perfect. I don't regret any of those difficulties, I've learned a lot.

What was very interesting was the exchange of knowledge. Both Ronan and myself were totally immersed in that project. We worked through osmosis. Ronan's initial ideas evolved along with our collaboration. He consulted me, asked me if it was possible to do one thing or another. Sometimes we erased everything or went further, refining the form.

Working with Ronan is a pleasure. It's always a joy to meet passionate people. My job allows me to earn my livelihood and I pursue it with passion - it's the best thing you can do. And that's rare.

88
« Torique » placemat
1999
Gilles Peyroulet Gallery,
France

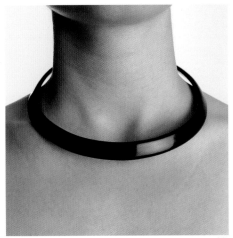

89   90

89
« Torique » coat hook
1999
Gilles Peyroulet Gallery,
France

90
« Torique » necklace
1999
Gilles Peyroulet Gallery,
France

91
« Torique » collection
1999
exhibition at the Grégoire
Gardette Gallery, Nice

6
DEPARTMENT STORES

For a company, selling is the final stage in the processing of an object. As the ultimate goal, it does a certain amount to inform the project as it develops. We're concerned with this question, and at the same time it's physically distanced from us. Once the project has passed the last stage of its development, companies take responsibility for commercialization. For some, like Habitat who sell through their own chain of stores, the context is quite clear, while for others, like Teracrea, distribution is based on department stores that are often characterized by their diversity. In spite of everything, throughout the whole of the project, we pay a lot of attention to the issues of commercialization. Often simple rules are laid down, connected, for example, to ease of storage. Sometimes, through a more elaborate scenario, and our efforts to understand and respond to the wants and desires of consumers, a project can evolve into a truly useful solution.

We designed the « Aio » collection for Habitat: a porcelain dinner service, complete from the cup to the plate. Fairly traditional in its craftsmanship, it aims to provide a certain practical quality. Using a system of standardized diameters, it allows the user to stack up different saucers, plates and bowls to create monolithic cylinders. The design is purposely kept fairly simple, in an inversion of what is traditionally the case with refined porcelain. Perhaps this collection is more for everyday use, less precious.

The Authentics « Fruit Bowl » is an attempt to refine a simple, inexpensive object. One of the concerns of Authentics was to be as distinctive as possible within the very competitive market of plastic objects. Often the quality and price are pretty much identical from one manufacturer to another. Our design was based on the use of two contrasting plastics: a translucent, grained polypropylene and an opaque and shiny ABS. Not much, just doing a bit more to mark the identity of an object distributed on a mass-scale.

The Cappellini « Fruit Bowl » rests on its slats. The fruits placed in it can breathe.

Our flower pots try to propose solutions for plant life within the modern habitat. The fountain provides constant humidity to the three pots that it supplies with water. The « Hanging Trellis » suggests a wall of plants. Terracotta cylinders are suspended from straps, and metal crosspieces serve as supports.

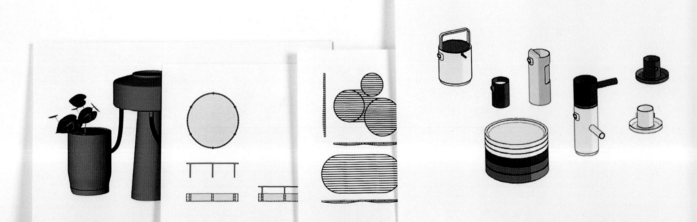

92

92
« Aio » collection of
porcelain crockery
2000
Habitat, England

93

94

93-94
« Aio » collection of
porcelain crockery:
coffeepot, cup, mug,
sugar bowl with lid and
spoon, teapot
2000
Habitat, England

95
« Aio » collection of
porcelain crockery:
coffeepot, cup, mug,
teapot, jug, milk jug,
shallow dish, soup dish,
pudding plate, bowl
2000
Habitat, England

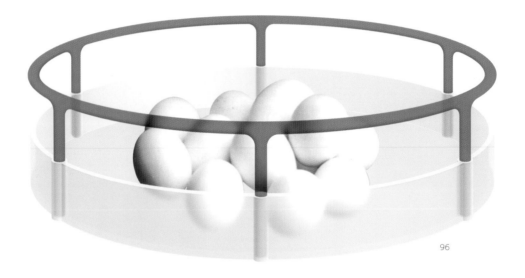

96

96
« Fruit Bowl »
collage
1999

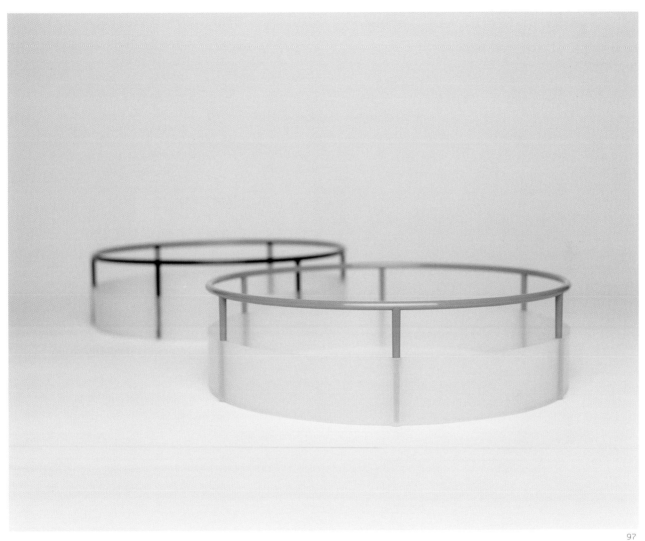

97

« Fruit Bowl »
1999
Authentics, Germany

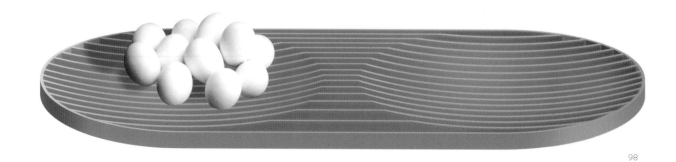

98

98
« Fruit Bowl »
collage
2001

99
« Fruit Bowl »
2001
Cappellini, Italy

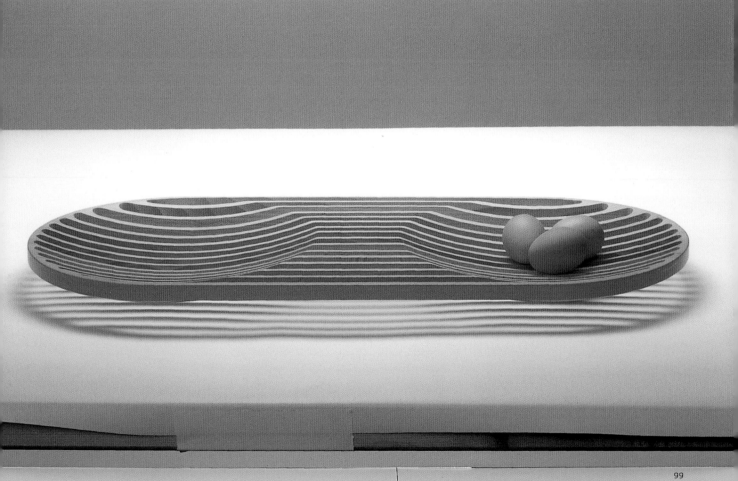

101

100
« Hanging Trellis »
detail
2003
Teracrea, Italy

101
« Fountains » clay pots
and water tank
2003
Teracrea, Italy

102 →
« Small Fountain » clay pots
and water tank, detail
2003
Teracrea, Italy

103-104 →
« Large Fountain » clay pots
and water tank, detail and
cross-section
2003
Teracrea, Italy

DEPARTMENT STORES | 81

7

TEMPLATES

We draw on sketch pads, or pile up sheets of paper. We work on several projects at the same time, some only in their initial stages, others being retouched for the last time.

A sketch can have any scale that you wish to give it. Often, as you run through a sketch pad, a line may represent one centimetre of a piece of plastic, then on the following page it can signify one metre of a piece of polystyrene. The sketchbook is the collection of different work contexts, from industry to craft, large-scale to small. And so, from one page to the next, one drawing simply guided by the hand can evolve from a piece in polystyrene to a well-crafted jewel.

The polystyrene « Clouds » and the jewels are both born of the same logic: they are the proliferation of a shared abstract form, like a growing plant, stubbornly repeating its structure of nodes. The clouds are designed to grow in an architectural space. Jewels rest on the skin.

The project of a wall for a shelter is based on the multiplication of a tiny three-dimensional motif. This piece, which resembles a small branch, is injected in polypropylene. Simply, with different colours and various alternate connections, we have managed to create an irregular skin. In this instance the repetition generates a certain visual complexity.

105

105-106 →
« Cloud » modules
2002
installation at the Musée
du Grand Duc Jean,
Luxembourg

107

108

109

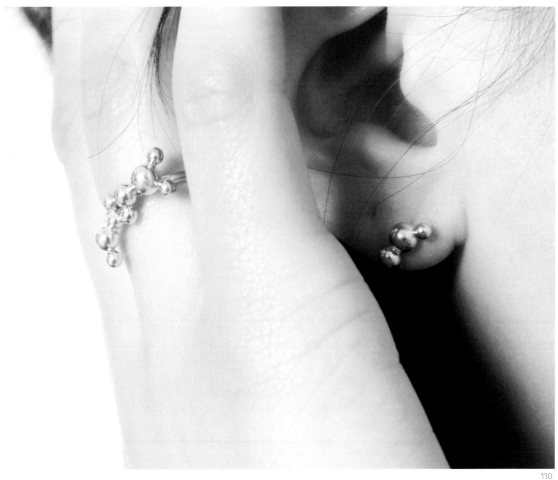

110

107
« Cloud » modules
maquette, cardboard,
paper, ink-jet print

108
« Cloud » modules
maquette, felt on rhodoid

109-110
« Cloud » ring and
earrings
2003
Biegel, Germany

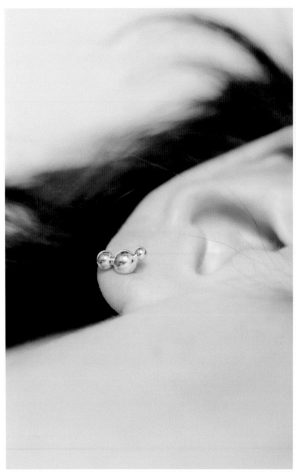

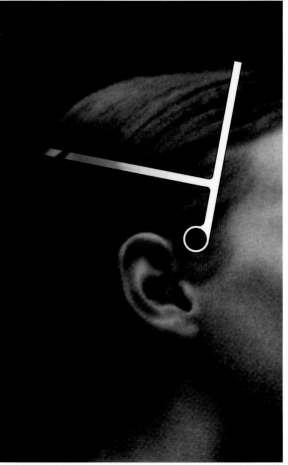

111

112

111
« Cloud » earring
2003
Biegel, Germany

112
« Serre-tête » headband
1999
Jenks/Smak, Iceland

113

113
« Necklace »
1999
Jenks/Smak, Iceland

BETC

The commission was simple: shelters were to be placed on a roof terrace to protect against sun and wind. The view is magnificent, Paris with zinc roofs.
Any hint of language on the architectural scale seemed to be ruled out as far as we were concerned. We just wanted to melt into the mass, to disappear, to allow the panorama to guide the eye. We concentrated on the skin of these shelters, bearing in mind that the cabins would be simple volumes, box-like structures. The skin is composed of a small unit of polypropylene, endlessly juxtaposed on supporting cables. The plastic allowed us first of all to make a piece that was easy to clip together, and also to play on the colours and its transparency.
As with a branch, « BETC » is not very far away from camouflage. An almost vegetable skin, it's chaotic when you approach it, but it can melt, through its blend of colours, into this greyish-blue mosaic of Paris rooftops.

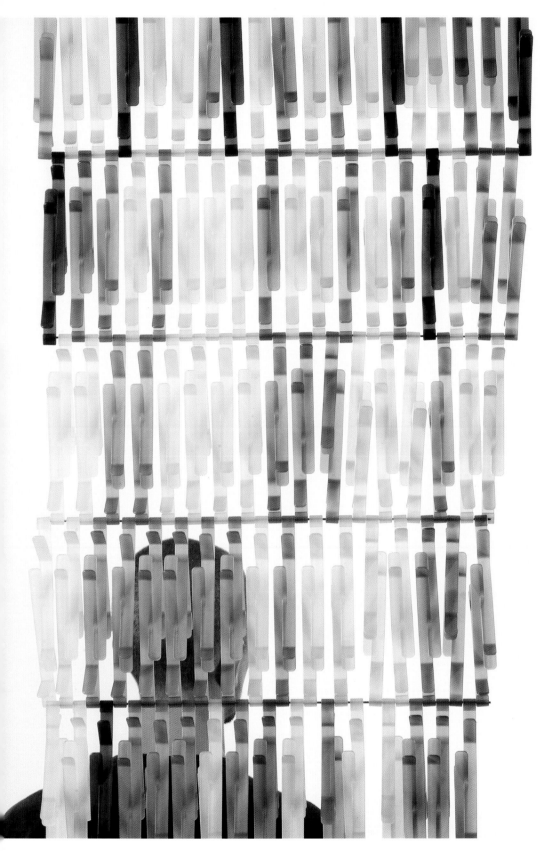

114-115
« BETC » wall system
2002

8
STILL LIFE

We're interested in beauty. It's a complex subject: to forget about function, to produce an object solely for the eye. A still life.

The still life is built in two dimensions. First of all it is based on formal qualities of proportions and colours. Secondly, it works through more cultural, symbolic referents. The doubt lies in reaching a finished image.

The green or blue « Vase » is in the first instance an alcove, a hollow volume. It holds a flower and, as in religious statuary, the « Vase » is a frame in which everything is controlled: background, light and colour. It means seeing a flower, almost deified: seeing it perfectly and seeing only that.

The candles carry the history of the ritual of wine, of welcome, as an image of benevolence.

←
Erwan Bouroullec,
« Untitled »
oil on canvas
1998

116
« Untitled » single-flower
vase, collage
1997
Ewans and Wong, France;
1998
Cappellini, Italy

116

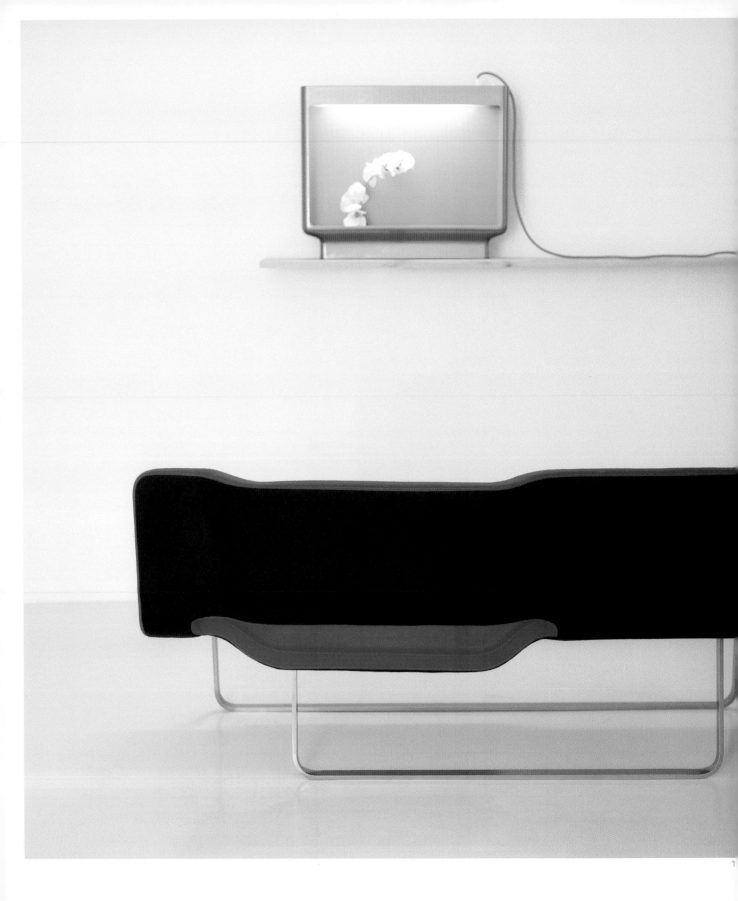

119

← 117
« Vase »
2001
Kreo Gallery, France
« Un et Demi » sofa
1999
Domeau & Pérès, France

← 118
« Vase »
2001
Kreo Gallery, France

119
« Candles »
1999
Backstage, France

120

121

Exhibition in the Cappellini
space in Milan, Italy 2003

120-121
« Butterfly » shelves
2002
Cappellini, Italy
« Vase» and « Honda Vase »
2001
Kreo Gallery, France

STILL LIFE

9
SOUNDS, LIGHTS

Both sound and light have this special quality of being impalpable, of having no visual essence. They are purely 'temporal' in the sense that they leave no trace of their passing. We are delineating components, emitters of light and sound, whose forms are essentially technical. Therefore we design a shell whose shape has to evoke an energy that it cannot contain. In this respect, a logic based on forms following functions (like a jug handle) goes out of the window.

Perhaps we should start with the « Parlo »: a trophy designed as the image of a victory that you must often conclude with a speech. Indeed, it is about giving a shape to something that is merely a recognition, trying to create an object that provokes a certain exuberance. This megaphone - being but a fascimile - is lined with felt like a piece of Hermès leatherwork.

The « Audiolab » is a commission for a specific kind of support. The question was quite simple: how best to allow people to hear sound-works in public spaces, particularly in art centres? Our answer was to construct a light roof from which the sound falls like rain. The 'fridge' on the side contains, both symbolically and practically, the machines that reassure us about the real source of the sound. The roofs contain speakers specifically designed for this particular configuration. The listener isn't imprisoned under this rain. The gaze slips away, distracting the eye and keeping the ear alert.

Where light is concerned, the shell is no longer merely a symbolic representation. It is often the very interface that serves to soften it, or on the contrary, to concentrate it.

The « Objets Lumineux » are big lamps, formed from a plywood skeleton which supports two half-shells of translucent thermoform plastic. These shells diffract the light, softening and diffusing it in all directions. There's this idea that technology should be invisible. Electronics follows the dogma of miniaturization, and you often expect this disappearance of technological objects towards a more immaterial use. Perhaps the oversized lamps were reacting to this myth. Giving them a human scale, a certain rather gentle presence is achieved in spite of everything.

The « Acrylic Lamps » are simply a skeleton, a formal definition of the boundaries of the light source.

122

123

124

125

124-125
« Parlo » trophy, collage
1999
International Festival of
Arts and Fashion
Hyères, France

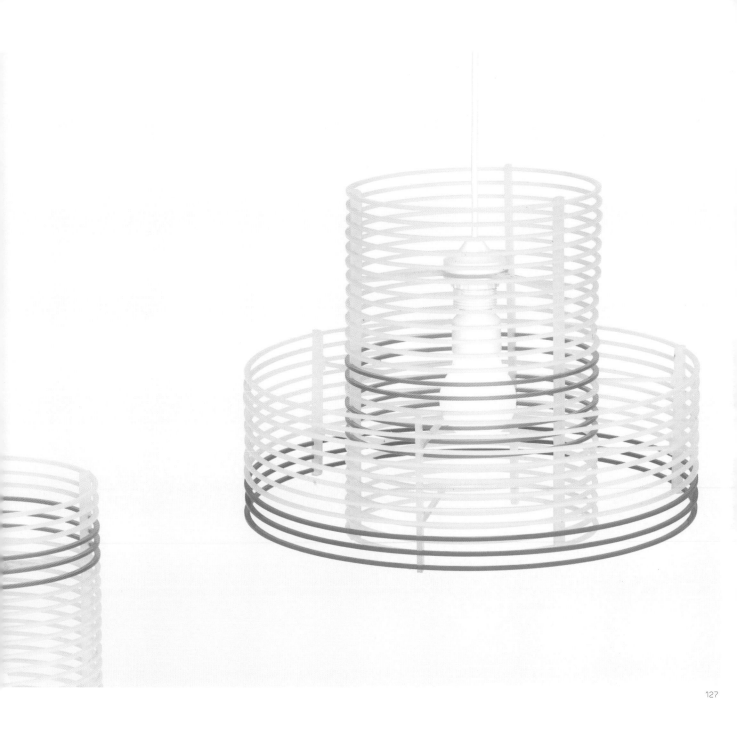

126-127
« Acrylic Lamps »
2001
Cappellini, Italy

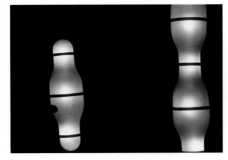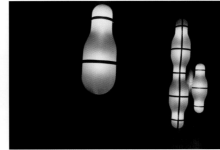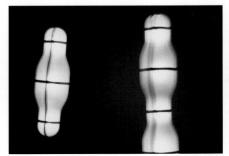

Luminaire
installation
1998
Saint-Étienne, France

128-129
« Objets Lumineux »
lamps
1999
Cappellini, Italy

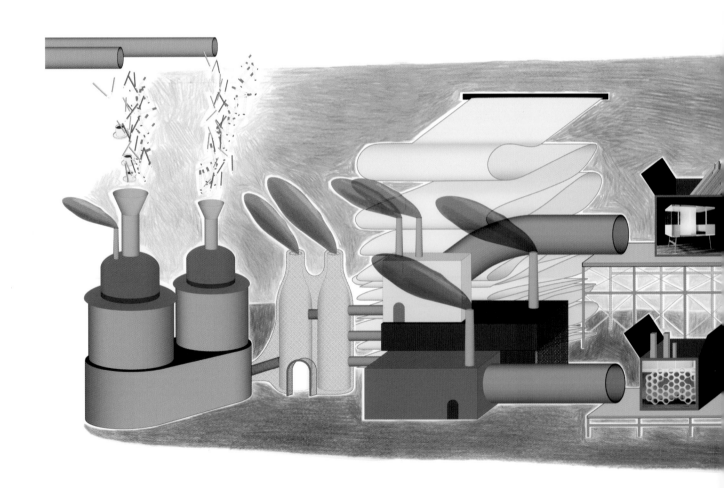

SOUNDS, LIGHTS

10
SITUATIONS

A situation is played out just as much in accordance with our mood as with our material surroundings. Sometimes our work is concentrated more specifically around the attention that we pay to the user. On the one hand an object is guided by its functionality, on the other, its typology often contains certain rituals and habits. Often the mere suggestion or accentuation of a prehensile quality, or the use of a material charged with history, allows us to go beyond a functional situation in order to attain a kind of *savoir-vivre.*

The « Valise » is a filing system with a lid and a handle attached. A label juts out. Between real issues of practicality and a reminder of our habitual behaviour, the « Valise » attempts to indicate a certain use: protecting, shifting and classifying.

The « Desk » is made of Corian® and leather. The Corian® is smooth, deep, rather cold. The desk blotter is made of leather, a fine sheet laid into the desktop's surface. With this surface, the touch oscillates between hard and supple, between the plain synthetic material and the leather.

Finally, the « Glide » sofa is harder to appreciate; at first glance it seems to be overly designed. In fact it combines a number of functions, as though it had contracted within itself a living room situation: a little set of shelves, a sofa, a chaise longue. A classic typology is supplemented by its close referents, in return for extra room and a certain fluidity of behaviour.

This chapter doesn't discuss multifunction. Rather it tries to evoke the way in which hand and body balance between the functionality of tool use and more sensitive reactions, linked to culture.

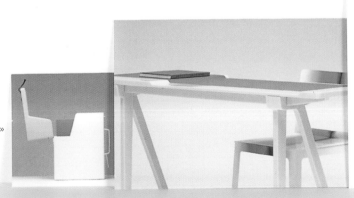

←
« The Bouroullec Factory »
pencil on computer
rendering

130

131

130
« Glide » sofa
2001
Cappellini, Italy

131
« Glide » sofa
maquette, cardboard and
fabric

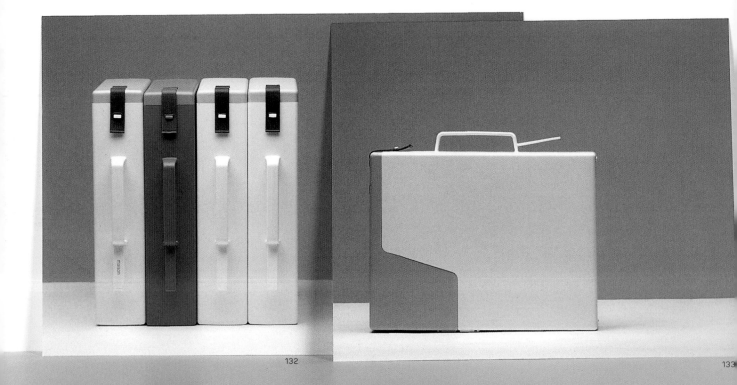

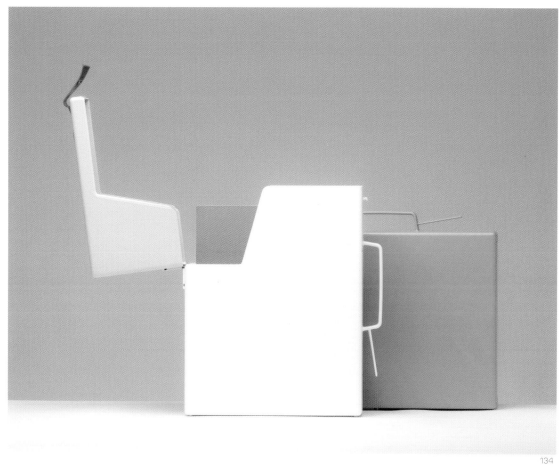

134

132-134
« Valise »
Filing system
2003
Magis, Italy

135-136
« Corian Desk »
2001
Domeau & Pérès, France

11
JAPAN

We were contacted by Issey Miyake, who commissioned the design of a space in Paris dedicated to his new clothes collection, A-POC. At first we thought that there was some mistake: until then our work had been restricted to furniture and objects.

The A-POC project bears all the marks of this situation. It was constructed not from the space to the detail, but rather from the detail to the space. First we designed the hangers, then a support for the hangers, and so on. That process was aimed at the creation of an array of tools that would allow Issey Miyake to play with the image of his space over time. Unlike a demonstrative proposition in terms of architecture, we substituted an evolutionary system that tends to disappear behind the clothes.

It's sometimes said that our work evokes Japan. Of course it speaks of it with an unchecked, distant gaze. But it is, perhaps, rather a western impression of simple and ethereal objects that has evoked this connection. The « Square Vase » effectively suggests a particular way of organizing the flowers one-by-one, in line with the idea that we might have of ikebana. But all these relationships remain imagined because we've never thought of our objects as a direct reference to Japanese culture.

We're sometimes asked about our influences and the effects they have on our work. We certainly integrate a kaleidoscopic range of images, and the cultural situations that we've encountered, but it seems to us that our work doesn't function through direct commentary.

137

137
« Square Vase »
1999
Cappellini, Italy

138

138-139
« A-POC Boutique »
views of the shop
2000
Issey Miyake, Paris

139

141

142

140-142
« A-POC Boutique »
views of the shop
2000
Issey Miyake, Paris

The A-POC space in Paris was conceived of as a support: to carry the clothes and accessories of a collection that changes and evolves every six months. The very open principle allows the space to have a different image over the course of time. The framework is a Corian® structure that runs along the walls and the ceiling. It is composed of three horizontal bars, a traditional one at the height of a clothes rail, one higher and one lower. The ceiling is criss-crossed with bars that primarily serve to carry the clothes on hangers. The heads of the hangers are hidden at the back of the bar. Then, a series of accessories, which are also placed on the framework, allows you to arrange other elements in a different way: big vertical metal plaques act as boards to which the clothes have been attached with magnets; horizontal plates hold clothes laid out flat, and also shoes or bags. Finally a play of little coloured plaques enables a form of punctuatation for the whole arrangement, allowing a distinction between the different ranges.

The curtains of the changing rooms are made up of a set of upholstered strips. They make the space of the changing rooms gentler, almost sound-proofed.

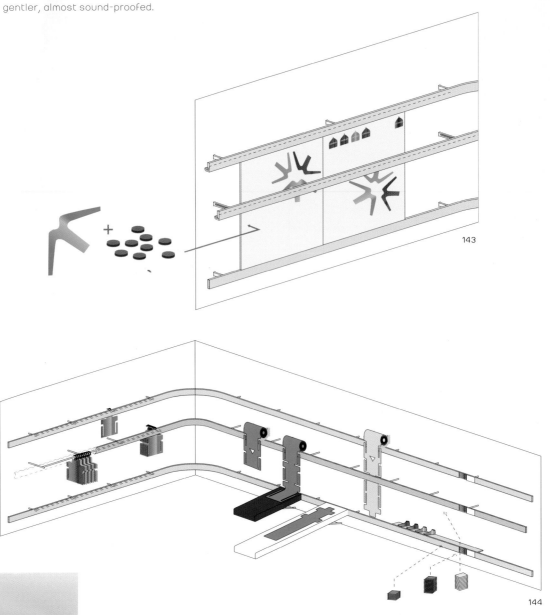

143

144

145

146

147

An encounter with any work by the Bouroullec brothers
is an essay on just how liberated design can be. Their
designs are unusually free from preconceived notions and
from the pressure of following a set convention. They are
not only universal and contemporary, but are also endowed
with vitality and delicacy; qualities that only ideas born out
of the rich soil of culture and history can achieve.

    Ronan and Erwan are a breath of fresh air in the world of
design.

ronan & erwan bouroullec
ロナン＆エルワン・ブルレック

bouroullec@wanadoo.fr
T +33 1 48 21 04 02 / F +33 1 48 21 04 60

Destiny

When Ronan met Giulio Cappellini for the first time, he didn't
yet have a business card. At the end of the meeting, Giulio,
holding out his own, concluded that it was better that way,
and that Ronan would risk no longer having any ideas once
he had one.

    Written in stone. Prophecy. As a matter of fact we still
don't have one.

    The Japanese card above is the only exception. We were
opening an exhibition in Tokyo when Issey Miyake learned
that we didn't have any cards. A big Japanese hoo-ha.
Three hours later we were able to join in the ritual of card-
exchange that presides over any conversation.

    We've still got them, just in case.

← 143-144
extract from the film « A-
POC »
explanation of the
system of presentation

← 145
part of the changing
room curtain, wool and
foam rubber
← 146
basket, drawing
← 147
piece of Corian®

148
« A-POC Boutique »
view of the shop
2000
Issey Miyake, Paris

12
MONOCHROME

Traditionally, the materials of the objects surrounding us are chosen and organized around their ability to respond to particular needs. It's often a fairly complex matter to find a single material that is capable of responding to all the requirements of the object. We have designed pieces in such a way that they are monochrome, their visible material is plain. Choosing uniformity makes the object simpler for the eye and erases the details. Strangely, this has the effect of rendering it all the more undefined.

The consoles are made entirely from Corian®. This synthetic material can be glued invisibly, allowing you to create the impression of a single, carved block. The same material also forms a vase or a mirror, running from the top all the way to the base. Thus everything is unified, the table with the vase, the mirror with the console.

Monochrome is a way of connecting uses and different limitations, linking both the technological and the habitual.

The « Butterflies » are large painted boxes. They become wardrobes, shelves, a storage space. In a single colour, they first of all try not to evoke materials that would confine them to one particular purpose or another and they also set out to be a mere support when, after a few years, they are filled with objects.

The « Corian Wardrobe » is a shell, an outline. When you put clothes in it, the hangers disappear. The clothes are simply surrounded by a frame of uncertain function, without proportion.

The single-flower vase is one of our first projects. It's a shape defined by an uninterrupted line, like a sketch.

In the beginning, a drawing is always an intention, with few details. Only afterwards does it become progressively more formalized. Monochrome is a way of remaining at a more fundamental stage of the idea.

149

15

151

150
« Console with Vase
and Bowl »
2001
Cappellini, Italy

151
« Console with Mirror »
2001
Cappellini, Italy

152 →
« Console with Mirror »
detail showing mirror

153→
« Console with Vase
and Bowl »
detail showing bowl

154

155   156

157

← 154-155
« Butterfly » shelves
details showing boxes
2002
Cappellini, Italy

← 156
« Butterfly » shelves
model in cardboard,
paper, ink-jet print

157-158
« Butterfly » shelves
2002
Cappellini, Italy

159

160

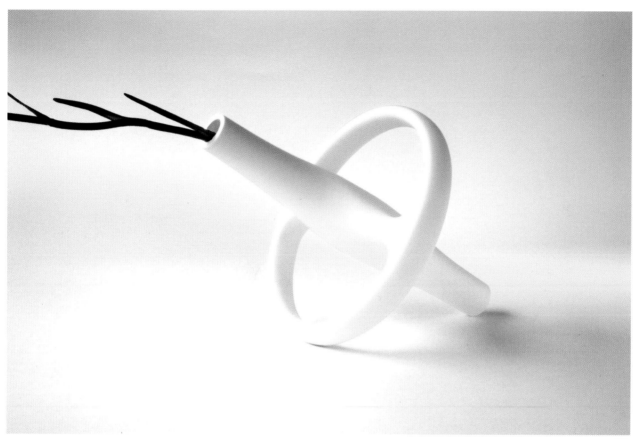

161

159
« Hole Chair » first
prototype
1999
Cappellini, Italy

160
« Hole Chair »
maquette,
Scotch®

161
« Untitled » single-flower
vase
1997
Ewans and Wong, France;
1998
Cappellini, Italy

13
SKIN

Skin is the surface of the object.

While the materials around us are becoming increasingly standardized and finishes are becoming more and more uniform, work on skin strikes us as being of prime importance. It allows you to intrigue the eye, making the perception of an object stranger than it would be if you were able to read its form and material in a simple manner.

We started by painting the « Hole Chair ». It is made of aluminium, cut out, folded, soldered. The painted shade of the green chair disturbs the vision. It appears like a ray of light on a shining object and creates a permanent weird reflection, having the effect of a *trompe-l'oeil*.

The name of the « Honda Vase » is a reference to the particular paint that we used, actually originating from the Japanese company. The vase has two surfaces, one of which has no thickness: hyper-shiny and metallic. The other surface adds depth to the hollow of the object: it's matt, it swallows light, creating a black hole.

We're not particularly interested in decor. We were rather thrown by Sommer's proposition: to create a motif for carpet tiles, 50 x 50 cm, to cover a floor. Certainly the result is formal, but this sequence of lines, when the pieces are placed together, causes the boundaries between the carpet tiles to disappear and the effect somewhat resembles a chess board. Here, skin serves to coalesce, to unify.

It's almost the same game with the project for the dinner service for the Prefecture of Strasbourg. It concerns how one connects different objects that are, moreover, made up of different materials.

And then there's the mirror, a reflection-object.

Coromandel Centrepiece

Here the material itself is nothing more than a colour reference. We are close to things that speak to the eye by diverting it from what they are in terms of production, quality of material, or richness - whether real or otherwise.
For walnut and mahogany we have substituted a sensation of colour, a coloured shadow.
Our intention was to create an opposition between an immaterial object and that which is most incarnate - food, something that can be weighed, cut and tasted.

162
« Centrepiece »
2001
Coromandel, France

163

164

163
Shade-selections, David
Toppani's studio,
Montreuil, France

164
Mr Toshiro Kawase
creating a floral
installation, « Ronan and
Erwan Bouroullec »
exhibition, Issey Miyake
Design Studio Gallery,
Tokyo
2001

165
« Hole Chair »
2000
Cappellini, Italy

166

167

168

166-168
« TV Mirror » mirror
2002
De Vecchi, Italy

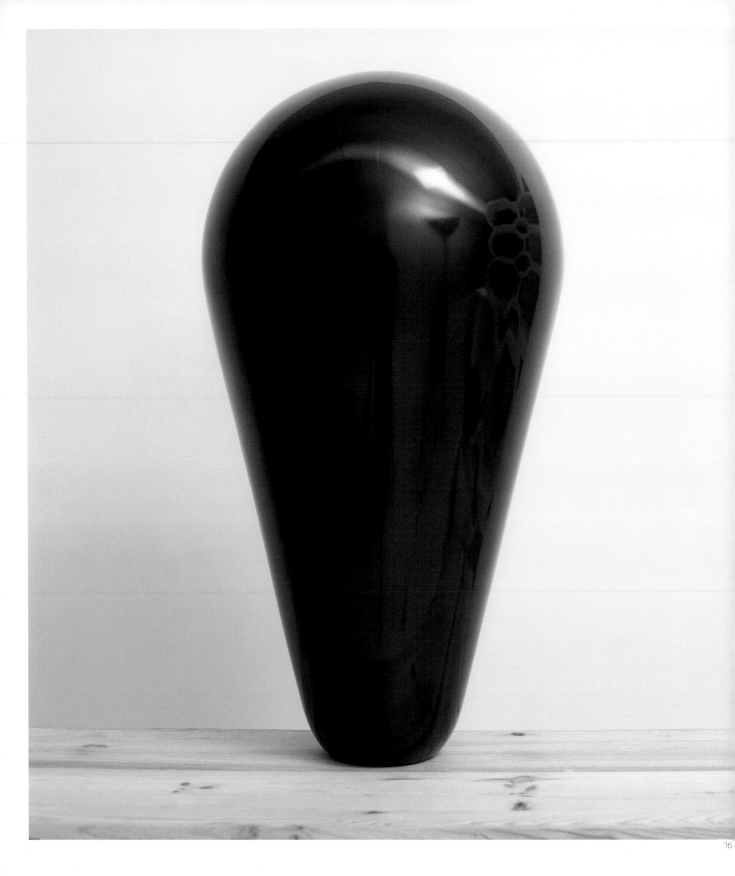

16

171

172

We were asked to design a porcelain dinner service for the Prefecture of Strasbourg: the different plates, a tablecloth, vases, and so on, but the project was never realized. The whole thing is a game for the gaze where you try to lose your eye in reflections and similarities.

The edge of the plates have two symmetrical wings. Under the superior, and hidden from view, is a printed solid colour, with a light rim that mingles with the reflection of the solid colour on top of the inferior. So the eye sees two hues of the same density: one direct, the other reflected.

The tablecloth was printed with a shade that suggests a dark circle, a centrepiece. The vases, candlesticks and porcelain bowls have a continuation of that colour enamelled on their base. While the whole set is connected when you look at it gently, it comes apart under scrutiny.

Ultimately, the dinner service relies upon inebriation, in a final doubling game, to lead the eye to doubt itself.

173

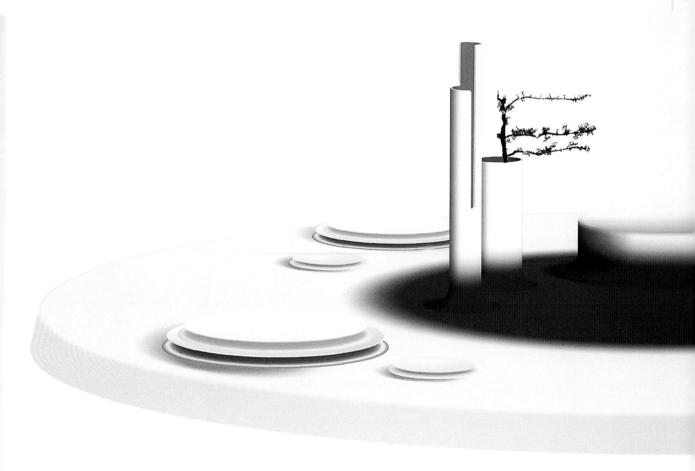

SKIN

14
ASSEMBLY

Being able to assemble pieces yourself often means being able to make decisions, to assess your real needs.

Primarily we're interested in ease of assembly because it forms the basis of the future of an industrial project. For a set of shelves, for example, this is fundamental in terms of the logistics of manufacturing and distribution. This ease of assembly, along with modularity, opens up an area of autonomy for the user, which isn't there with pieces that are complicated to build. Simplicity of construction forces you to go back to simple gestures, to common sense, to a universal skill.

The « Charlotte » shelves consist of plates moulded in fibreglass and sheets of glass. You put the first plate on the ground, fasten the glass sheets of your choice into its grooves, position the next plate, and so on.

The two carpets also require simple actions: you assemble little units. To get away from the traditional surface of a rug, the « Zip » uses zip fasteners. It suggests infinite length, the user decides on its dimension and colour composition. The « Tapis Grappe » is organized by simple juxtaposition. Here it can equally well produce a surface or a path, its perimeter being completely free.

As to the « Polystyrene House », it requires no skill in the sense that all the steps required are quite obvious. *A priori*, it can be assembled by anyone at all, with a minimum of organization.

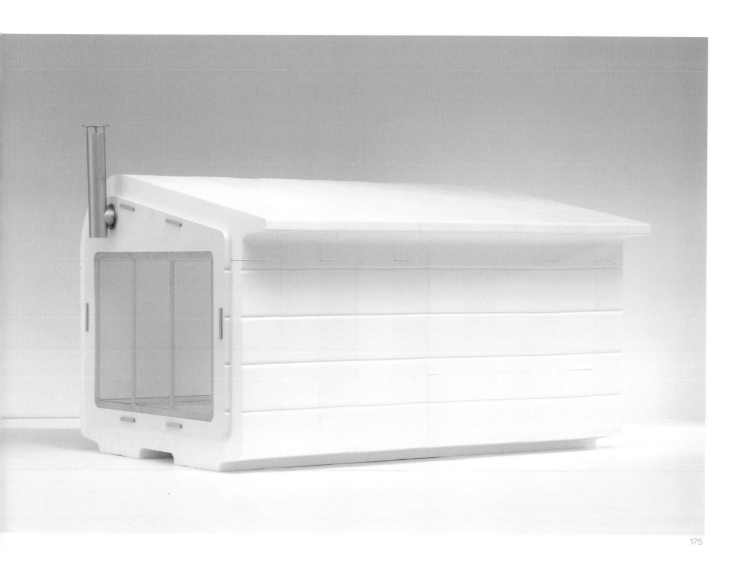

175
« Polystyrene House »
maquette
2002

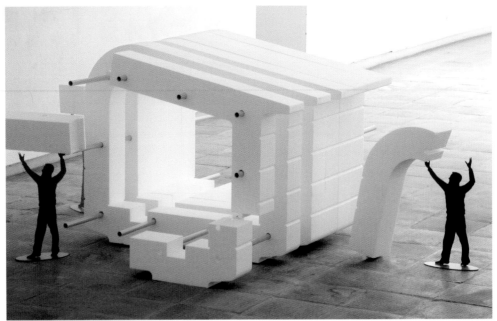

176

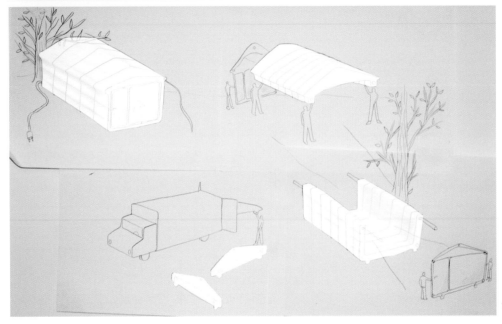

177

The Polystyrene House

The « Polystyrene House » is built up of polystyrene strips, two facades made of wood and glass (including the door and windows), and a wooden floor placed on the polystyrene. Each polystyrene strip is taken from a series of eight interlocking pieces that are cut out according to a numbered sequence, then assembled and slipped over supporting tubes. The surface of the house depends on the number of strips you decide to install. When the strips are assembled, the house is practically finished: it presents itself in the form of a tunnel. Then you put a wooden floor down on the polystyrene and close the tunnel at each end with the two wood and glass facades, including the door and windows.
The technical casing for the water and electricity are contained within the wooden floor.

176
« Polystyrene House »
exhibition: Des petites
maisons interessantes à
habiter (Small houses that
are interesting to live in),
Villa Noailles, Hyères,
France 2002

177
« Polystyrene House »
drawing of house
assembly

178
« Polystyrene House »
maquette, polystyrene,
plywood, painted PVC,
rubber, string, Plexiglas®
2002

179

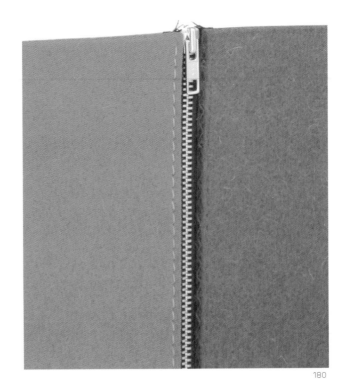

180

179-181
« Zip Rug »
2001
Cappellini, Italy

181

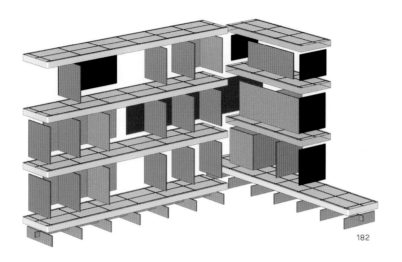

182

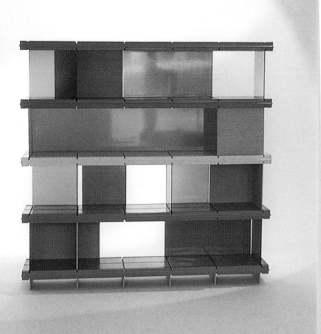

182
« Charlotte » shelves,
drawing

183
« Charlotte » shelves
2000
Neotu Gallery, France

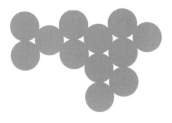

184-185
« Tapis Grappe » rug
2001
Kreo Gallery, France

15
WALLS AND A ROOF

Taking the « Lit Clos » bed and the « Disintegrated Kitchen » as our starting-point, we embarked upon research in which we increased the traditional scale of furniture .

This research is primarily articulated around the formation of walls and, more generally, around those elements that structure the space. While the bed and the kitchen were still more specifically function-based projects, we gradually found ourselves coming closer to more indistinct designs relating to walls and roofs. Work on this scale actually implies a certain restraint. We are very critical of proposals that attempt to cover all the functions of a given situation.

These projects just try to create sensitive boundaries: being beside, behind, below. They aim to give the space a feeling, a direction, to make the user more sensitive to a particular place. And so the function of these places don't belong to us.

The « Parasol Lumineux » lamp attracts people just as a hearth does when you walk into a home. The feeling of finding yourself below a roof, which is itself below a ceiling, attracts and brings people a greater intimacy. The space is created by an immaterial context, connected with that sense of 'being below'.

The « Cabane » simply defines a perimeter, and thus an inside and outside, because it escapes typologies suggesting a particular use, returning to the simple idea of the boundary.

Our technical culture isn't the same as that of architects. In these designs we've transferred a skill connected with furniture-making, in that we're using 'light' techniques. Light, when you bear in mind that after all a sofa arrives complete, in a cardboard box. Light because they don't require a particular skill on the part of the user, unlike the more traditional materials and machinery of building work. Ease of assembly is fundamental, giving the user a certain autonomy, even on this scale.

As to the « Clouds », the « Suspended Trellis », the « Cabane », it may be that our work operates on the level of a series of motifs, on the creation of various different motifs for the domestic environment. It is a simple reaction against the tendency towards uniformity in the quality of the walls, floors and roofs that surround us.

Following this path has led us to a complete yet floating house. So it remains an unanchored object, it could be located elsewhere.

186

Ronan and Erwan
Bouroullec Exhibition
2001
Kreo Gallery, Paris

186
« Brick » polystyrene
module
2000
Kreo Gallery, France
« Cabane »
2001
Kreo Gallery, France

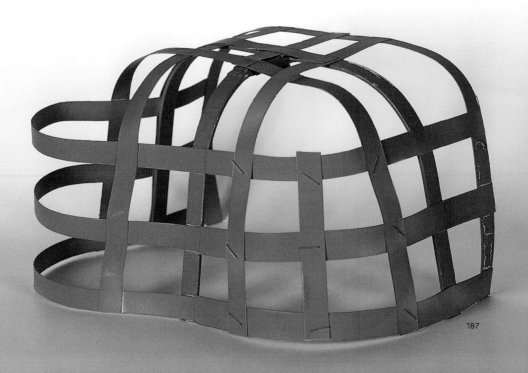

187

187
« Cabane »
maquette, paper,
aluminium and staples

188
« Cabane »
2001
Kreo Gallery, France

189

190

Brick

The polystyrene shelves are cut out with a laser. We had originally conceived these elements as the backdrop for an exhibition. Our plan was to avoid having to remake backdrop elements on every site using traditional techniques. Moreover, we wanted to perfect a sort of brick that was easy to assemble, capable of being adapted to different configurations, and above all that was of a 'standard' quality.

This turns the laser principle into something like a big printer. The file leaves our studio, the manufacturer performs the cut-out process and then delivers the pieces. Polystyrene-cutting is a technology that you can find anywhere in the world, meaning we're able to produce pieces near the sites where our exhibitions are being held.

191

189
« Ronan and Erwan
Bouroullec » exhibition,
Issey Miyake Design
Studio Gallery, Tokyo
2001

190
« Ronan et Erwan
Bouroullec » exhibition,
Design Museum, London
2002
study maquette, ink-jet
print, paper, cardboard,
Sellotape®

191
« Brick » polystyrene
module
2000
Kreo Gallery, France

192

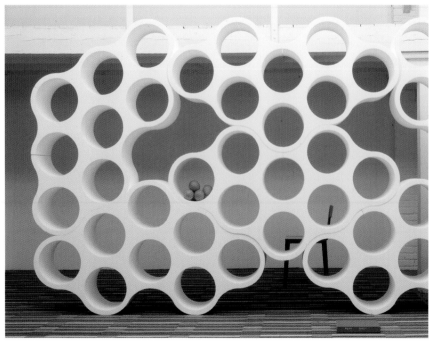

193

192
« Hanging Trellis »
2003
Teracrea, Italy

193
« Cloud » module
2003
Cappellini, Italy

194
« Parasol Lumineux »
lamp
2001
Kreo Gallery, France

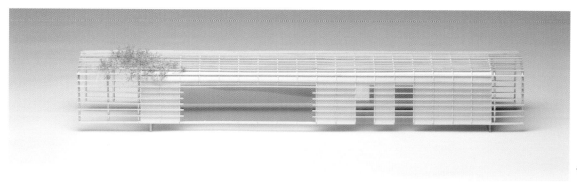

196

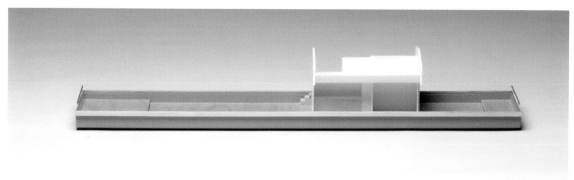

197

The Floating House

It's a floating studio house designed as a place for an artist in residence. You can both live and work in it. Life and work are articulated around different spaces, neither defined nor definitive. A few items of furniture are arranged within it. The « Floating House » consists of a barge and some polyester bars (like the skin of a boat) assembled to make the wall and the roof. Two glazed facades open up on to the terraces and the river. A wooden trellis covers and dresses the whole of the house. The vegetation that will grow over it tends to integrate the building within the tree-lined landscape of the shores, and allows the residents to preserve their intimacy.

This project has been realized in collaboration with the architects Denis Daversin and Jean-Marie Finot.

195-197
« Floating House »
maquette of PVC,
aluminium, Plexiglas® and
wood
2002
Centre d'Art de Chatou,
France

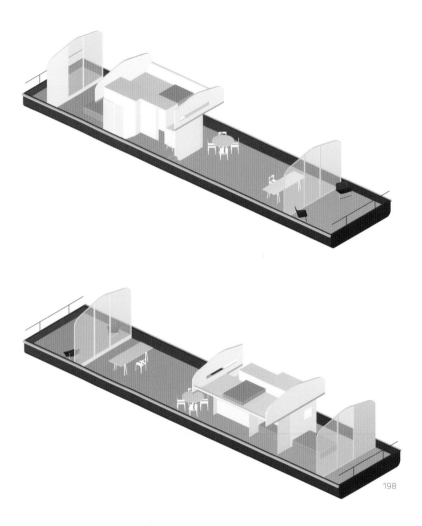

198

198
« Floating House »
drawing
axonometric and internal
organization

199
« Floating House »
maquette

200
« Floating House »
drawing

16
PERIPHERIES

For two years we've been going back and forth to Marseilles, to the Cirva, a glass research centre. Their aim is to put sophisticated tools and high-level glass technicians at the disposal of visual artists or designers, and through that collaboration to arrive at new approaches to glassmaking. The working situation here is very different from the those we usually encounter: there is no concrete definition of objectives, no imperative to get a result and the studio is open to us with no time limit.

Our approach consists in seeking new ways of using glass. For the time being it isn't a matter of object or function. We compact powder, we sew, we develop modes of assembly. We make a large number of samples a few centimetres square and expose them to different intensities of heat, compiling an index of results - methodically rather than scientifically.

Glass is a highly seductive material - you have to keep it at arm's length when you're working with it, if you wish to try and suggest new directions. If certain of our experiences proved to be blind alleys, others seem to carry the promise of concrete applications. Starting out from this range of procedures, we are now trying to define their use. The absence of directives makes the exercise puzzling, but that's why its so interesting.

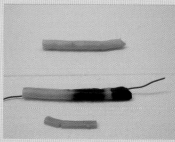

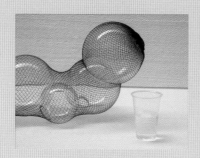
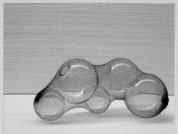

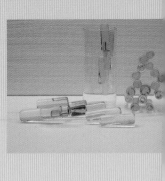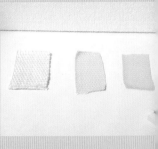

202

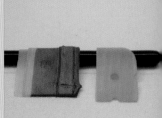

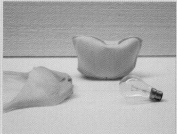

203

←201, 202, 203
« Recherches »
2002-2003
Centre international
de recherche sur le verre
et les arts plastiques,
Marseille, France

17
STONES

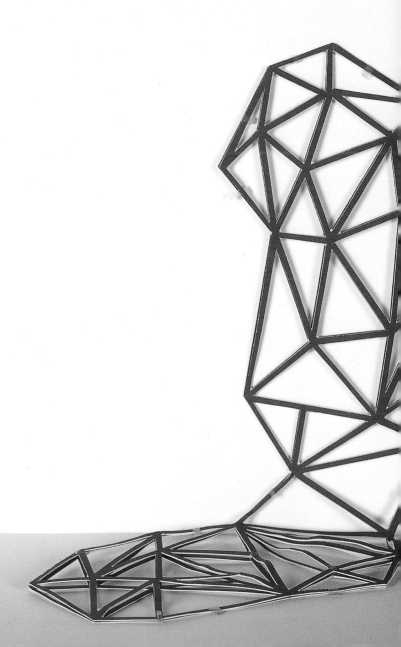

Sometimes we escape our usual working environment. The Kreo Gallery in Paris, with whom we work, gave us this chance; over many years we have established a great collaboration with its director, Didier Krzentowski. Other opportunities to open exhibitions present themselves, such as « Blossoming Gap » with Andrea Branzi at the Rendel & Spitz Gallery in Cologne. The gallery is not part of the same kind of market as a manufacturer. It has no factory, no terms and conditions. It's very close to contemporary forms of art and allows unique pieces of work outside of the usual framework.

The problem facing us is much like that of the blank page, a strange situation for those of us who are attached to the idea of context, of dialogue. But this work, like the one described in the previous chapter, is actually a source of direction. A place where you wander down paths that are less well defined, but which nonetheless feeds our whole work. Having sprung directly from our sketchbooks, these designs are more suggestive than may be immediately apparent.

204

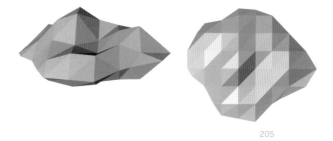

205

204
« Stones » vase
2002
Plastic Arts Delegation,
Ministry of Culture
France

205
« Stones » vase
drawing

206

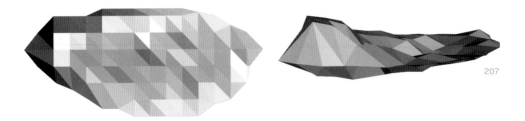

207

206
« Stones » bowl
2002
Plastic Arts Delegation,
Ministry of Culture,
France

207
« Stones » bowl
drawing

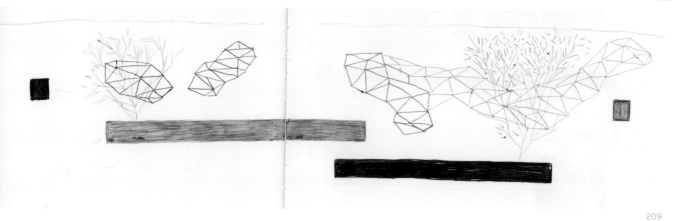

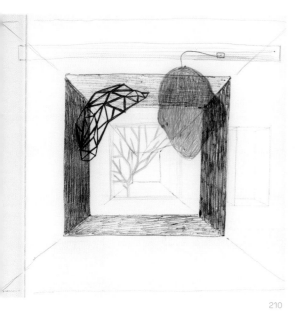

Blossoming Gap
exhibition
Andrea Branzi, Ronan
and Erwan Bouroullec
2003
Rendel & Spitz Gallery,
Cologne

208
« Blossoming Gap »
« Rock » detail

209-210
« Blossoming Gap » study
drawings

The twenty-first century is starting slowly, with no general plans or unique models of development. After a long period of violent transformations and revolutions (the twentieth century), brought about by mechanics and its search for strong symbols and final solutions, a new era begins, marked by endless waiting and progress without any single purpose.

Let us leave behind us the powerful and concentrated cathedrals of the old modernity, let us start instead to use on-line cognitive processes and to bring about environmental transformations both reversible and silent. Our modernity is a new modernity capable of transforming the weak and diffuse energies of nature; energies that do not produce the uproar of mechanics but, as stars and planets do, can lift up all the oceans of the world, every night, and without making a sound.

The concept of 'weakness' we are referring to does not suggest any flaw; on the contrary it suggests new forms of perception and transformation of the world, following diffuse processes, reversible strategies, crossable perimeters and 'fuzzy' logic rather than geometrical. It suggests the virtue of modesty and caution enshrined in all those imperfect and incomplete models that follow elastic strategies and can therefore grasp the new, as well as face the unexpected (including the complexity that descends from it).

And so a new modernity comes to life, closer to nature and to the constant innovations nature generates; it follows the climatic, genetic and geological energies of agriculture, and is able to produce serial flowers, those redolent gardens where technology reaches the zenith of its aesthetic performance.

Zygmunt Bauman tells us of a Liquid Modernity that does not possess a form of its own but tends to follow a temporal flow of transformations. This modernity becomes its own sole judge, pursuing its own modernization. It realizes paradigms where individual freedom coincides with all the liquefaction processes of the general system.

This ultimate coincidence of subject and system, individual and society, brings about a new definition of a metropolis as a large genetic deposit: an urban reality where architecture establishes nothing but a weak connective system linked to a pile of human presence, relationships, interests and interchanges that fill the space entirely.

Therefore the metropolis of the computerized age is not a capital of technology, but rather a humanness territory, in its full ability to connect its DNA to that of others, within an economy of interchange and the spreading of trade. The deep and light energy of a tree feeds all the technologies, both aesthetic and structural, of a new architecture.

213

211
« Blossoming Gap »
study drawings

212
« Blossoming Gap »
exhibition catalogue

213
« Blossoming Gap »
exhibition detail

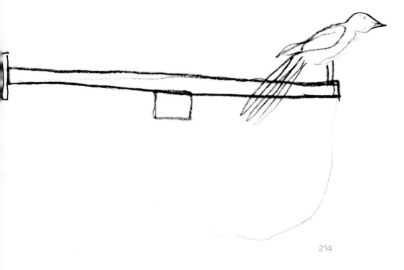

214

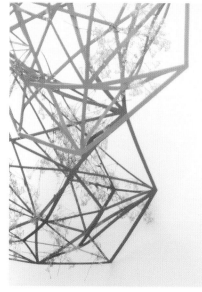

214
« Blossoming Gap »
study drawing
2003

215-216
« Blossoming Gap »
detail
2003

List of Works

1
IN THE BEGINNING
p 7 Erwan Bouroullec, painting, 1997
oil on canvas

1, 5-6 Disintegrated Kitchen, 1998
aluminium, wood, plastics
main unit : 90 x 220 x 70 cm/ 35 x 86 x
27 in
prototype developed with the help of
a grant from the VIA
Cappellini, Italy

2-4 Lit Clos, bed, 2000
painted birch plywood, steel, aluminium,
thermoform Altuglass®, fabric
200 x 240 x 140 cm/ 78 x 93 x 54½ in
base 70 cm or 180 cm/ 27 in or 70 in
off the floor
prototype developed with the help of
a grant from the VIA
limited edition of twelve copies,
including two artists' proofs, signed
and numbered
Kreo Gallery, France

7-9 Hole Collection, 1999
wall fixture, birch plywood, glass
• console 80 x 124 x 32 cm/ 31 x 48½ x
12½ in
• shelf 126 x 124 x 32 cm/ 49 x 48½ x
12½ in
• shelf 185 x 124 x 32 cm/ 72 x 48½ x
12½ in
• table 75 x 90 x 90 cm/ 29½ x 35 x 35
in
• table 75 x 180 x 90 cm/ 29½ x 70½ x
35 in
• table 75 x 220 x 90 cm/ 29½ x 85½ x
35 in
prototype developed with the help of
a grant from the VIA
Cappellini, Italy

2
MULTIPLES
10-15 Combinatory Vases, 1997-1998
eight pieces, polyurethane, variable
dimensions
prototype developed with the help of a
grant from the Fonds d'Incitation à la
Creation (FIACRE), Délégation aux Arts
Plastiques
Neotu Gallery, 1997, France
Cappellini, 1998, Italy

16-17 L'Eau d'Issey, line of scented
body products, 2002
packaging, polypropylene, glass
• scented bath and shower gel,
200 ml - 16 x 11.5 cm/ 6 x 4½ in
• moisturising body cream,
200 ml - 16 x 11.5 cm/ 6 x 4½ in
• scented deodorant
100 ml - 16 x 5 cm/ 6 x 2 in
• soothing scented night cream
100 ml - 20 x 7 x 2.5 cm/ 8 x 3 x 1 in
• alcohol-free scented roll-on deodorant
75 ml - 16 x 6.5 x 3.5 cm/ 6 x 2½ x 1½ in
Beauté Prestige International for
Issey Miyake, agent Kreo

18 Coffee Cup n 4, 1998
porcelain, 5 x 12 x 6 cm/ 2 x 5 x 2 in

prototype, unrealized project

3
FIVE SEATS
19-21 Outdoor, 2001
armchair with or without head-rest,
with or without cushion (layer of
polyurethane and polyester),
polystyrene sheets, polyurethane foam,
PVC, matt chrome steel base
three colours: black, white or grey
two versions:
• with head-rest, 100 x 78 x 69 cm/ 39
x 30½ x 27
• without head-rest, 72 x 78 x 69 cm/
28 x 30½ x 27 in
Ligne Roset, France

22-24 Safe Rest, daybed, 1999
wool blanket, foam, cotton, zip
fastener, steel
two versions :
• 45 x 240 x 80 cm/ 17½ x 94 x 31 in
• 45 x 240 x 160 cm/ 17½ x 94 x 62½ in
Domeau & Pérès, France

25-27 Spring Chair, 2000
shell of wood, then polyurethane, high-
resilience foam, wool, stainless steel
four versions:
• armchair
66 x 78 x 78 cm/ 26 x 30½ x 30½ in
• armchair + foot-rest
66 x 78 x 120 cm/ 26 x 30½ x 47 in
• armchair + head-rest
90 x 78 x 86 cm/ 35 x 30½ x 33½ in
• armchair + foot-rest + head-rest
90 x 78 x 130 cm / 35 x 30½ x 51 in
Cappellini, Italy

28-30 Hole Chair, 2000
painted aluminium
Five colours: white, green, white and
blue/purple shades, shades of green
and white, white and pink/blue shades
73 x 45 x 45 cm/ 28½ x 17½ x 17½ in
Cappellini, Italy

31-32 Samouraï, armchair, 2002
shell of dense polyurethane foam,
fabric, stainless steel base
63 x 52 x 43 cm/ 24½ x 20¼ x 17 in
Cappellini, Italy

4
FACTORIES
33-75 Joyn, office system, 2002
mixed materials and techniques
• platforms, dimensions variable
• benches, dimensions variable
• organizational tools, dimensions
variable
• micro architecture :
- canopy 252 x 430 x 140 cm/ 94 x 168
x 54½ in
- talkpoint 180 x ø 80 cm/ 70 x ø 31 in
- bay 162 x 100 x 100 cm/ 63 x 39 x 39 in
Vitra, Switzerland

5
A WORKSHOP
76-83, 85, 86, 88-91 Torique Collection,
1999

• jug, turned enamelled ceramic
42 x ø 8 cm/ 16½ x ø 3 in
• table, moulded enamelled ceramic
42 x ø 50 cm/ 16½ x ø 19½ in
• vase, turned enamelled ceramic
12 x ø 80 cm/ 5 x ø 31 in
• oil lamp, turned enamelled ceramic
25 x 14 cm/ 10 x 5½ in
• stool, turned enamelled ceramic
45 x 42 x 22 cm/ 17½ x 16½ x 8½ in
• bowl, turned enamelled ceramic
10 x 36 cm/ 4 x 14 in
• placemat, turned enamelled ceramic
5 x ø 22 cm/ 2 x ø 8½ in
• coat hook, turned enamelled ceramic
20 x 15 cm/ 8 x 6 in
• necklace, turned enamelled ceramic
ø 18 cm/ ø 7 in
the collection as a whole was
commissioned by the Direction
Régionale des Affaires Culturelles de
Provence-Alpes-Côte-d'Azur,
Ministère de la Culture, and the town
of Vallauris
Gilles Peyroulet & Cie Gallery, France

6
DEPARTMENT STORES
92-95 Aio, collection of porcelain
crockery, 2000
• soup dish, ø 24 cm/ 9½ in, white
• salad bowl, ø 24 cm/ 9½ in, white
• flat dish, ø 24 cm/ ø 9½ in, white, blue
and grey
• cafetière with filter 600 ml, white
• cup 7 x 6.5 cm/ 3 x 2½ in, white
• cup saucer, 1.7 x 13 cm/ 1 x 5 in, white
• mug 11.2 x 7.3 x 11.5 cm/ 4½ x 3 x 4½
in, white
• mug saucer, 2 x 15 cm/ 1 x 6 in, white
• sugar-bowl with lid and spoon
7.6 x 14.5 cm/ 3 x 6 in, white
• milk-jug 11.5 x 7 x 8 cm/ 4½ x 3 x 3 in,
white
• pudding plate, ø 14.5 cm/ ø 6 in,
white, blue and grey
• bowl ø 14.5 cm/ ø 6 in, white, blue and
grey
Habitat, England

96-97 Fruit Bowl, 1999
polypropylene, ABS
8.2 x ø 30 cm/ 3 x ø 12 in
Authentics, Germany

98-99 Fruit Bowl, 2001
solid wood
two versions:
• 4 x ø 28 cm/ 1½ x ø 11 in
• 4 x ø 65 cm/ 1½ x ø 25½ in
Cappellini, Italy

100-101 Hanging Trellis, 2003
terracotta, Nylon® and steel
two versions:
• 12 x 69 x 100 cm/ 5 x 27 x 39 in
• 12 x 69 x 220 cm/ 5 x 27 x 86 in
Teracrea, Italy

101-104 Fountains, 2003
terracotta, rubber
two versions:
• ø 67 x 110 cm and 47 x 40 x 54 cm/
ø 26 x 43 in and 18 x 15½ x 21 in
• ø 33.5 x 55 cm and 23½ x 20 x 27 cm/

ø 13 x 21.5 in and 9 x 8 x 10½ in
Teracrea, Italy

7
TEMPLATES
105-108 Cloud, module, 2002
polystyrene
105 x 187.5 x 40 cm/ 41 x 73 x 15½ in

109-111 Cloud, 2003
• ear-rings, platinium
15 x 5 x 9 mm/ ½ x ¼ x ½ in
• ring, platinium
22 x 10 x 20 mm/ 1 x ½ x 1 in
Biegel, Germany
112 Serre-tête, headband, 1999
steel sheet, laser cut
four versions:
• 10 x 15 x 4.3 cm/ 4 x 6 x 2 in
• 10 x 15 x 13 cm/ 4 x 6 x 5 in
• 12 x 15 x 2.5 cm/ 5 x 6 x 1 in
• 13 x 15 x 1.5 cm/ 5 x 6 x ½ in
Jenks / Smak, Iceland

113 Necklace, 1999
steel sheet, laser cut
12 x 15 x 2.5 cm/ 5 x 6 x 1 in
Jenks / Smak, Iceland

114-115 BETC, wall system, 2002
polypropylene
20.9 x 8.6 x 2.5 cm/ 8 x 3½ x 1 in
a shelter was conceived on behalf of
the agency Euro RSCG-BETC

8
STILL LIFE
p. 97 Erwan Bouroullec, Untitled, 1998
oil on canvas

116 Untitled, single-flower vase, 1997
ABS injected,
20 x ø 14 cm/ 8 x ø 5½ in
Ewans et Wong, 1997, France
Cappellini, 1998, Italy

117-118, 120-121 Vase, 2001
stratified polyester, matt internal finish,
external finish paint and shiny
bodywork varnish, removable lid
incorporating a fluorescent light source
with dimmer
two colours: blue or green
52 x 66 x 15 cm/ 20 x 26 x 6 in
limited edition of twelve copies,
including four artists' proofs, signed
and numbered
Kreo Gallery, France

117 Un et Demi, sofa, 1999
shell in fibre glass and polyester resin,
high-resilience foam, wool blanket,
base in painted steel
80 x 155 x 80 cm/ 31 x 60½ x 31 in
prototype developed with the help of a
grant from the VIA
Domeau & Pérès, France

119 Candles, 1999, wax
29 x 27 x 20 cm/ 11 x 10½ x 8 in
Backstage, France

120-121 Butterfly, shelves, 2002
aluminium honeycomb, stratified

coating shaded by computer program
two versions :
• 220 x 107.5 x 60 cm/ 86 x 42 x 23½ in
• 220 x 125 x 60 cm/ 86 x 49 x 23½ in
Cappellini, Italy

121 Honda Vase, 2001
stratified polyester, matt internal finish,
external finish paint and shining
bodywork varnish, ballasted base
two versions: aubergine or black
100 x ø 50 cm/ 39 x ø 19½ in
limited edition of twelve, including four
artists' proofs, signed and numbered
Kreo Gallery, France

9
LIGHTS, SOUNDS
122-123 Audiolab, sound system,
2002
steel, polyester, fabric,
player/amplifier, audio speakers
200 x 440 x 408 cm/ 78 x 171½ x 159 in
First model commissioned by the
Caisse des Dépôts et Consignations
Kreo Gallery, France

124-125 Parlo, trophy 1999
polypropylene, felt
19 x 32 x 15 cm/ 7½ x 12½ x 6 in
Festival International des Arts de la
Mode de Hyères, France

126-127 Acrylic Lamps, 2001
Plexiglass®
three versions:
• table lamp 31 x ø 22 cm/ 12 x ø 8½ in
• ceiling lamp 31 x ø 22 cm/ 12 x ø 8½ in
• ceiling lamp 31 x ø 40 cm/ 12 x ø 15½ in
Cappellini, Italy

128-129 Objets Lumineux, lamps,
1998-1999
birch plywood, thermoform Altuglass®,
fluorescent bulbs
three versions:
• ø 50 x 120 cm/ 19½ x 47 in
• ø 50 x 160 cm/ 19½ x 62½ in
• ø 50 x 240 cm/ 19½ x 94 in
prototype École des Beaux-Arts
de Saint-Étienne, 1998, France
Cappellini, 1999, Italy

10
SITUATIONS
p. 114-115 The Bouroullec Factory, 2003
pencil on computer rendering,
artist project commissioned by Tate
Gallery, London

130-131 Glide, sofa with or without
foot-rest, 2001
expanded polyurethane stuffing, fabric
or leather covering, stainless steel base
two versions:
• with foot-rest, 85 x 245 x 140 cm/
33 x 95½ x 54½ in
• without foot-rest, 85 x 245 x 114 cm/
33 x 95½ x 44½ in
Cappellini, Italy

132-134 Valise, filing system, 2003
ABS, Hytrel®, Nylon®
three colors: green or grey with orange

catch; grey or white with grey catch
37 x 8 x 31 cm/ 14½ x 3 x 12 in
Magis, Italy

135-136 Corian Desk, 2001
Corian® structure, desktop covered
with leather
76 x 145 x 76 cm/ 29½ x 56½ x 29½ in
limited edition of one hundred, signed
and numbered
Domeau & Pérès, France

11
JAPAN
137 Square Vase, 1999
ceramic
5 x 40 x 40 cm/ 2 x 15½ x 15½ in
Cappellini, Italy

138-148 A-POC Boutique, Paris, 2000
Corian®, painted metal, wool, resin,
polyurethane, surface 120 m²/ 390 Ft²
Issey Miyake, agent Kreo Gallery

12
MONOCHROME
149 Corian Wardrobe, 2001
Corian®
180 x 220 x 40 cm/ 70¼ x 86 x 15½ in
Cappellini, Italy

150, 153 Console with Vase and Bowl,
2001
Corian®
55 x 200 x 45 cm/ 21.5 x 78 x 17½ in
Cappellini, Italy

151-152 Console with Mirror, 2001
Corian® and mirror
80 x 200 x 45 cm/ 31 x 78 x 17½ in
Cappellini, Italy

154-158 Butterfly, shelves, 2002
aluminium honeycomb, stratified
covering shaded by computer program,
two versions:
• 220 x 107.5 x 60 cm/ 86 x 42 x 23½ in
• 220 x 125 x 60 cm/ 86x 49 x 23½ in
Cappellini, Italy

159, 160 Hole Chair, prototype, 1999
fibre glass, painted plastic
73 x 45 x 45 cm/ 28½ x 17½ x 17½ in
Cappellini, Italy

161 Untitled, single-flower vase,
1997-1998
injected ABS
20 x ø 14 cm/ 8 x ø 5½ in
Ewans et Wong, 1997, France
Cappellini, 1998, Italy

13
SKIN
162 Centrepiece, 2001
metal, bodywork paint
4 x ø 40 cm/ 1½ x ø 16 in
limited edition of twenty-one copies
Coromandel, France

165 Hole Chair, 2000
painted aluminium
five colours: white, green, white and

blue/purple shades, shades of green
and white, white and pink/blue shades
73 x 45 x 45 cm/ 28½ x 17½ x 17½ in
Cappellini, Italy

166-168 TV Mirror, mirror, 2002
polished silver
30 x 40 x 8 cm/ 12 x 15½ x 3 in
De Vecchi, Italy

169-170 Honda Vase, 2001
stratified polyester, matt interior
finish, exterior finish paint and shining
bodywork varnish, ballasted base
two colours: aubergine or black
100 x ø 50 cm/ 39 x ø 19½ in
limited edition of twelve, including four
artists' proofs, signed and numbered
Kreo Gallery, France

171-172 Piece of Carpet, 1999
acrylic, PVC
50 x 50 cm/ 19½ x 19½ in
Sommer, France

173-174 Strasbourg Dinner Service,
2002
porcelain
dish, plate, vases, candlesticks, bowl,
bread dish, silk-screen tablecloth
unrealized project

14
ASSEMBLY
175-178 Polystyrene House, 2002
polystyrene, plywood, PVC,
rubber, strings, Plexiglas®
129.5 x 170 x 98 cm/ 50½ x 66 x 38 in

179-181 Zip Carpet, 2001
composable elements, wool felt, zip
fastener,
five colours including pumpkin, green
and sea-blue
dimension of an element 200 x 75 cm/
78 x 29 in
Cappellini, Italy

182-183 Charlotte, shelf with variable
configurations and dimensions, 2000
polyester resin, fibre glass,
screen-printed glass, laquered MDF
• plate: 6 x 220 x 41 cm/ 2 x 86 x 16 in
• glass panels: 28 x 34.8 x 0.8 cm/ 11
x 13½ x ¼ in, 28 x 70.4 x 0.8 cm/ 11 x
27½ x ¼ in, 37 x 34.8 x 0.8 cm/ 14½ x
13½ x ¼ in, 37 x 70.4 x 0.8 cm/ 14½ x
27½ x ¼ in, 37 x 175 x 0.8 cm/ 14½ x 68
x ¼ in
• assembled panels, laquered MDF:
37 x 35.6 x 34.8 cm/ 14½ x 14 x 13½ in,
37 x 87.4 x 34.8 cm/ 14½ x 34 x 13½ in
• base: 10 x 220 x 40 cm/ 4 x 86 x 15½ in
Neotu Gallery, France

184-185 Grappe Carpet, 2001
velvet 100% pure Woolmark wool,
weaving of a single piece
three colour gradations: blue, green or
grey
surface: 84 cm²/ 33 in², thickness:
2 cm/ ¾ in
limited edition of one hundred copies
signed and numbered
Kreo Gallery, France

15
WALLS AND A ROOF
186-188 Cabane, 2001
plastic and metal structure, cover
wool blanket,
colours: green interior and khaki
exterior
180 x 390 x 200 cm/ 70¼ x 152 x 78 in
limited edition of five including two
artist's proof, signed and numbered
Kreo Gallery, France

186, 189-191 Brick, module, 2000-2001
polystyrene, laser cut
50 x 300 x 40 cm/ 19½ x 117 x 15½ in
realized as a backdrop for the exhibition French Shoes at the Festival
International des Arts de la Mode de
Hyères, 2000, France
Kreo Gallery (polystyrene), 2001, France
Cappellini (wood), 2001, Italy

192 Hanging Trellis, 2003
terracotta, Nylon®, steel
two versions:
• 12 x 69 x 100 cm/ 5 x 27 x 39 in
• 12 x 69 x 220 cm/ 5 x 27 x 86 in
Teacrea, Italy

193 Cloud, module, 2003
polystyrene,
105 x 187.5 x 40 cm/ 41 x 73 x 15½ in
Cappellini, Italy

194 Parasol Lumineux, 2001
circular metal base, two fluorescent
tubes with dimmer
colour: white
200 x 186 x 186 cm/ 38 x 72½ x 72½ in
limited edition of five including two
artist's proof, signed and numbered
Kreo Gallery , France

195-200 Floating House, 2002-2003
PVC, aluminium, Plexiglas®, wood
359 x 2280 x 504 cm/ 140 x 889 x
196½ in
Project for the Centre National de
l'Estampe et de l'Art Imprimé (CNEAI),
Chatou, France, in the process of real-
ization, in collaboration with
Jean-Marie Finot and Denis Daversin

16
PERIPHERIES
201-203 Ongoing research for the
Centre Internaional de Recherché sur
le Verre et les Arts Plastiques
Marseille, France, 2002-2003

17
STONES
204-207 Stones, 2002
porcelain
• vase 9 x 16 x 18 cm/ 3½ x 6 x 7 in
• bowl 9 x 16 x 36 cm/ 3½ x 6 x 14 in
commissioned by the Délégation aux
Arts Plastiques, Ministère de la
Culture, France

Biography

Ronan Bouroullec was born on 13 June 1971 in Quimper, France. He studied at the Ecole Supérieure des Arts Décoratifs, Paris.
Erwan Bouroullec was born on 7 March 1976 in Quimper, France. He studied at the Ecole Nationale d'Arts de Cergy, France.

1992
Exhibitions
« La nouvelle vague des objetistes », Maison de la Culture de Chambéry
« VIA, les arts de la table », Roanne Theatre, France

1997
Exhibitions
« Dix ans de design français », Boulogne-Billancourt
« Made in France », Musée National d'Art Moderne, Centre Georges Pompidou, Paris
« OFF » with Matali Crasset, Space Carole de Bona, Paris
« Rémanence », VIA Gallery, Paris
« Vases combinatoires », Neotu Gallery, Paris
« Contenitori di solidi, di liquidi e di sogni », Abitare il tempo, Verona
« Homo Domus » organized by VIA, French Cultural Centre, Milan
« Paris-Milano » by the magazine *Intramuros*, Ara di Diogène Gallery, Milan
« Design with a French Twist », Feldman Gallery, Los Angeles
Awards and acquisitions
Mention du Jury de la Presse Internationale, Salon du Meuble de Paris
Acquisition of « Untitled » single-Flower vase by the Fonds National d'Art Contemporain (FNAC), France
Acquisition of « Untitled » single-Flower vase by the Musée National d'Art Contemporain, Centre Georges Pompidou, Paris

1998
Exhibitions
« La vie en rose », Fondation Cartier, Paris
« Objets lumineux », Exposition Biennale Internationale du Design, Saint-Étienne
« Trois designers trois artisans » with J F Dingjian and M Ruiz de Azua, La Chantrerie, Cahors, France
« Vases combinatoires », Villa de Noailles, Hyères, France
« Design with a French Twist », Neptunbad, Cologne
Awards and acquisitions
Grand Prix de la Critique de la Presse Internationale, Salon du Meuble de Paris
Grand prix du Design de la Ville de Paris
First prize, Biennale du Design de Saint-Étienne
Acquisition of « Vases combinatoires » by the Fonds National d'Art Contemporain (FNAC), France
Teaching
Ronan: assignment at École Nationale des Beaux-Arts de Nancy

1999
Exhibitions
« Minimal », Peyroulet & Cie Gallery, Paris
« Trois designers, trois artisans », Escola Massana, Barcelona
« Torique », Musée de la Céramique, Vallauris, France
« Torique », Grégoire Gardette Gallery, Nice
« Joint-venture », A T Kearney, Neuilly-sur-Seine, France
« A Grand Design », Victoria and Albert Museum, London
« French Design and New Material », Tokyo
« Index », Harajuku, Tokyo
Awards and acquisitions
New Designer Award, International Contemporary Furniture Fair, New York
Acquisition of « Torique » collection by the Fonds National d'Art Contemporain (FNAC), France
Acquisition of « Torique » collection by the Musée National de la Céramique, Vallauris, France
Teaching
Ronan: workshop, École Nationale des Beaux-Arts de Saint-Étienne

2000
Exhibitions
« Etat de siège », VIA Gallery, Paris
« Babybloom », Luisa Delle Piane Gallery, Milan
« Des arts plastiques... à la mode », Christie's/Beaux Arts, Paris
« Faces of Design », Museum of Modern Art, New York
« Design, Design », Villa Noailles, Hyères
Patricia Dorfmann Gallery, Paris
« Byob », Néotu Gallery, Paris
Gilles Peyroulet Gallery, Paris
Awards and acquisitions
Mention du Jury de la Presse Internationale, Salon du Meuble de Paris
Teaching
Ronan: teaching at the École Camondo, Paris and workshop at the École Cantonale d'Art de Lausanne, Switzerland

2001
Exhibitions
« Ronan and Erwan Bouroullec », Miyake Design Studio Gallery, Tokyo
« Manger, les nouveaux modèles d'habitation », Salon du Meuble, Paris
« Mutations », Musée des Arts Décoratifs de Bordeaux
Awards and acquisitions
Nomination Compasso d'Oro for the « Spring Chair », ADI
« Nombre d'or », prize awarded jointly to Ronan and Erwan Bouroullec and to Cappellini
Teaching
Ronan: teaching at the École Cantonale d'Art de Lausanne

2002
Exhibitions
« Ronan and Erwan Bouroullec », Design Museum, London
« Une petite maison intéressante à habiter », Villa Noailles, France
« Les nuages en polystyrènes », Issey Miyake installation, Yvon Lambert Gallery, Paris
« Audiolab », Palais de Tokyo, Paris
« Les nuages en polystyrènes », Musée du Grand-Duc-Jean, installation for the Museum Night, Luxembourg
« Joyn », office system for Vitra, Orgatec Fair, Cologne
« Joyn », office system for Vitra, Designer's Saturday, Lagenthal, Switzerland
Awards and acquisitions
Designer of the Year, *Elle Décoration* Design Awards, 2002, London
Acquisition of « Vase » by the Design Museum, London
Teaching
Ronan: teaching at the École Cantonale d'Art de Lausanne

2003
« Ronan en Erwan Bouroullec », Droog Design Gallery, The Netherlands
« Blossoming Gap », exhibition in collaboration with Andrea Branzi, Rendel & Spitz Gallery, Cologne
Awards and acquisitions
Créateur de l'Année, Salon du Meuble de Paris
Teaching
Erwan: workshop, École des Beaux-Arts de Bordeaux
Ronan: teaching, École Cantonale d'Art de Lausanne

Selective Bibliography

1991

Articles

• Thierry de Beaumont, « Ronan Bouroullec », *L'Atelier: Le Magazine de la création contemporaine*, n 5, January-February 1991

1993

Articles

• F M, « Ronan Bouroullec: un peu de poésie », *La Croix l'Evénement*, 16-17 May 1993, p 14

1997

Books

• Yoichi Nakamuta, « Ronan Bouroullec », *Le toolpub, les designers Maintenant!*, Fly, London, pp 15-19

• Pierre Staudenmeyer, «Dix ans de design en France », *Design français, l'art du mobilier : 1986-1996*, special issue Beaux-Arts magazine, Paris, 1997

Articles

• Elisabeth du Closel, « Paris: Ronan Bouroullec », *Maison Française*, 491, Winter 1997-98, p 28
• Bénédicte Duhalde, « Ronan Bouroullec, le design par hasard », *Intramuros*, n 68, December 1996-January 1997, p 38
• « Esprit d'objets », École Nationale Supérieure des Arts Décoratifs, *Journal des arts décos*, n 10, April 1997, p 18
• « Le design en France: l'actualité 1986-96 », *Le Courrier des métiers d'art*, n 161, April 1997
• Béatrice Loyer, « Ronan Bouroullec, un jeu combinatoire », *Techniques & Architecture*, n 435, December 1997, pp 58-59
• Nicole Michalon, « En attendant la biennale de design », *La Tribune Le Progrès*, n 46549, 22 November 1997
• « Résidence d'été d'artistes aux Arques: désignez-moi une résidence », *La Dépêche du Midi*, 15 August 1997
• Marco Romanelli, « Design, L'Europa dei giovani: Ronan Bouroullec », *Abitare*, n 365, September 1997, p 174

1998

Books

• *Cap 5, periodico di segni e immagini*, Cappellini, Milan, Spring 1998
• Christine Colin, ed. « Ronan Bouroullec: combinaisons », *Terminologie et Pataquès*, coll. « Les Villages », Industries Françaises de l'Ameublement / Hazan, Paris, 1998, p 41-47

Articles

• P A, « Blinder Formzoeten », *Architektur & Wohnen*, June 1998, pp 666-667
• Jean-Pascal Billaud, « Les 2000 combinaisons de Ronan Bouroullec », *Marie-Claire Maison*, n 338, December 1997-January 1998, p 54
• Jean-Pascal Billaud, « Ronan Bouroullec », *Marie-Claire Maison*, n 344, October 1998, p 36

• Stefania Bricchi, « Novità in produzione », *Interni*, n 472, July-August 1998, p 12
• Roberto Callegari, « Un centro di informazione e cultura », *Gapcasa, l'informazione al punto vendita*, n 143, March 1998, pp 56-57
• Michèle Champenois, « Ronan Bouroullec contre le vide minimaliste », *Le Monde*, 13 November 1998, p 27
• Annick Colonna-Césari, Michèle Leloup, Colombe Pringle, Martine Vincent, « Jeunes créateurs: ils donnent du style à notre vie », *L'Express le magazine*, n 2437, 19 March 1998, p 12
• « Création artistique et ergonomie des banques d'accueil et de prêt: le cas de la nouvelle bibliothèque de Fresnes », *Bulletin des Bibliothèques de France*, n 6, 1998, pp 4, 46-50
• « Cuisine désintégrée: Ronan Bouroullec », *AMC*, n 2552, June-July 1998, p 87
• Catherine Delbos-Ader, « Les Ultracontemporains », *DS*, n 11, April 1998, p 137
• Sophie Djerlal, « Blanc sur blanc », *Jalouse*, n 6, December 1997-January 1998, p 131
• Elisa Donel, « A pœsia do modulavel », *A & D (Arte e Decoraçao)*, n 224, September 1998, pp 22-23
• Bénédicte Duhalde, « La Combinatoire selon Ronan Bouroullec », *Intramuros*, n 74, December 1997-January 1998, pp 24-25
• Brigitte Fitoussi, « Francia '98-'99, Ronan Bouroullec », *Design Diffusion News*, n 65, December 1998, pp 86-89
• Brigitte Fitoussi, « Les cartes blanches du VIA », *L'Architecture d'aujourd'hui*, n 316, April 1998, pp 101-102
• Brigitte Fitoussi, « Design en intérieur », *De Architect*, November 1998, p 111
• Catherine Geel, « < OFF / ON > Ronan Bouroullec », *Jalouse*, n 8, March 1998, p 132
• Sophie Lemoine, « Ronan Bouroullec: le goût du modulable », *Le Figaro*, n 8 January 1998, p 19
• Sophie Lemoine, « Designer en devenir », *Maison française*, n 493, Spring 1998, p 39
• Christine Lippens, « L'esquisse et la main », *Maisons Côté Sud*, n 58, June-July 1998, p 31
• « Les Beaux Objets de Ronan Bouroullec », *Familles*, 3 May 1998, p 5
• Grazia Maffi, « Néotu: a new show room opened in Nice », *Design Diffusion News*, January-February 1998, p 73
• Catherine Maliszewski, Martine Vincent, « Cuisine: la nouvelle convivialité; "Techno nomade" », *L'Express le magazine*, 15 October 1998, p 16
• Enrico Morteo, « L'investimento della ricerca, Cucina destrutturata », *Interni*, n 479, April 1998, p 192
• Birgit Müller, « Ausgekocht & abgebrüht », *Design Report*, August 1998, p 60

• « New French Touch », *Elle Deco*, n 36, June 1998, p 98
• Nonie Niesewand, « Molto Tecno Milano », *Wallpaper**, n 12, July-August 1998, p 93
• Cécile Olivéro, « La cuisine de demain épurée et modulable », *Résidences décoration*, n 20, March-April 1998, p 127
• Jeanne Quéheillard, « Initiatives: L'histoire d'une commande », *Intramuros*, n 78, August-September 1998, pp 66-69
• Marco Romanelli, « L'alfabetiere del design », *Abitare*, n 375, July-August 1998, p 143
• Marco Romanelli, « 12 oggetti », *Abitare*, n 378, November 1998, p 155
• « Ronan Bouroullec », *Le Catalogue des créateurs en direct*, n 1, Spring-Summer 1998, p 7
• « Ronan Bouroullec, objets identifiables », *Azimut*, n 15, 1998, special Biennale Internationale du Design de Saint-Étienne, 7-15 November 1998, p 110
• « Salon du meuble de Milan 1998 », *Intramuros*, n 76, April-May 1998, p 54
• Catherine Scotto, « La Jeune Garde du design français », *Elle Décoration*, n 84, December 1998-January 1999, p 50
• Alexandra Senes, « Shopping, Vase composé », *Beaux-Arts magazine*, n 164, January 1998, p 21
• Christian Simenc, « Design à Saint-Étienne », *Marie-Claire Maison*, n 345, November 1998, p 50
• « Variation autour d'un vase », *Entrée en matières*, n 11, March 1998, p 5
• Martine Vincent, « Ronan Bouroullec, designer nomade », *L'Express le magazine*, 13 August 1998, p 7
• Gersende de Whitby, « Voglia di internazionalità », *Gapcasa, l'informazione al punto vendita*, n 143, March 1998, pp 53-55
• P Yanou, U Fulchiron, « Ronan Bouroullec: les envahisseurs », *Workshop*, n 13, Biennale Internationale du Design de Saint-Étienne, November 1998, pp 4-5

1999

Books

• Christine Colin, ed., *Confort et inconfort* coll. « Les Villages », Industries Françaises de l'Ameublement / Hazan, Paris, 1999, p 29, 96-97, 114-116, 118
• Brigitte Fitoussi, « Désir-fonctionnalité, identité: des choses et des mots », *L'Objet du design*, exhibition, 6-11 July 1999, Paris Design, Paris, 1999, p 54
• Brigitte Fitoussi, Christophe Pillet, « Ronan Bouroullec », in *Repères 99*, Salon du Meuble, Paris, pp 14-18 January 1999
• Jasper Morrison, ed., *The International Design Yearbook 1999* Laurence King Publishing, London, 1999, pp 114-117, 125-127, 158, 205

Articles

• Uta Abendroth, « Moderne Designer wollen alles, nur nicht dekorieren »,

Badisches Tagblatt, n 4, September 1999
• Uta Abendroth, « Die Suche nach Sachlichheit », *Pfetzheimer Zeitung*, n 28, August 1999
• « Are you the French Dickson, Ronan Bouroullec? », *Ahead*, Summer 1999, p 27
• John Arent, « Paris Furniture Fair: France's New Wave », *Blueprint*, n 158, February 1999, p 54
• « Avant-garde, Ronan Bouroullec », *Avant-garde*, December 1999
• Julie Borgeaud, « Décoration: chics et simples; meubles liberté », *Paris Match*, 19 February 1999, pp 96-98
• Christine Bottero-Lhardit, « Lits de repos simplissimes », *Elle*, n 2783, 3 May 1999, pp 270-271
• Clotilde Briard, « Ronan Bouroullec: il veut libérer les objets », *L'Usine Nouvelle*, 26 August 1999, p 23
• Jesse Brouns, « Eigengereed design », *Week end Knack, Special Wohnen*, n 13 October 1999, pp 114-119
• Denis Bruna, « Ronan Bouroullec, de l'industrie à l'artisanat », *L'Estampille l'Objet d'Art*, n 338, July-August 1999, p 16
• Annick Colonna-Césari, « Design: plastique pas toc! », *L'Express le magazine*, n 2525, 25 November 1999, pp 30-33
• « Deux designers à Vallauris », *Artstances*, July-August 1999, p 15
• « Deux designers à Vallauris », *Dizajn*, n 20, May-July 1999, p 7
• « Deux designers à Vallauris », *Le Courrier des métiers d'art*, n 182, July-August 1999
• « Deux designers à Vallauris », *Maison française*, n 501, September 1999, p 58
• *Dizajn*, n 21, September-November 1999, p 6
• *Dizajn*, n 22, December 1999, pp 5, 14
• « Douze créateurs, douze dessins, douze tonalités... et un seul support: la dalle textile!», *Le Monde de Sommer*, n 3, February 1999
• Véronique Dupont, « Talents hauts », *Numéro*, n 9, December 1999-January 2000, p 44
• Hélène Erena, « Un atelier - galerie », *Nice matin*, 18 July 1999, p 16
• Claire Fayolle, « Designers à Vallauris, le renouveau de la céramique », *Beaux-Arts magazine*, n 185, October 1999, p 14
• Anne-Marie Fèure, «Sans mobilier apparent», *Libération*, 4-5 December 1999, pp 42-43
• Brigitte Fitoussi, « Il Salone del mobile di Parigi, 1999 », *Design Diffusion News*, n 67, March 1999, pp 88-108
• Brigitte Fitoussi, « Paris fin de siècle, Ronan Bouroullec », *Design Diffusion News*, n 74, December 1999, pp 115-117
• Brigitte Fitoussi, « Néo crafts », *Numéro*, 5, July-August 1999, p 54
• Brigitte Fitoussi, « Next plus ultra », *Numéro*, 7, October 1999, p 66
• Isabelle Fougère, « Sonic House », *Tribeca*, 22, December 1999-January 2000, pp 32-35
• « François Bauchet et Ronan Bouroullec à Vallauris », *Revue de*

l'ameublement, n 7, September 1999, p 58
•« Vallauris, Bouroullec, Bauchet : l'esprit des formes », *Nice matin*, 12 September 1999, p 16
•Catherine Geel, « Ils créent la dalle », *Jalouse*, n 18, March 1999, p 20
•Laura Houseley, « Him Indoors », *Wallpaper**, March 1999, p 211
•*Interni International*, supplement to *Interni*, n 489, April 1999
•Gérard Laizé, « Futuroscopie, projection dans un futur incertain », *Citizen K international*, n 12, Autumn 1999, pp 73-77
•Karine Larqué, « Safe Rest », *Jalouse*, n 19, April 1999, p 153
•Nadia Lionello, « Oggetti in sintesi », *Interni*, n 491, June 1999, p 110
•Christine Lippens, « L'Esquisse et la main », *Maisons côté sud*, June-July 1999, p 74
•Béatrice Loyer, « La Fête du design à Saint-Étienne », *Techniques et architecture*, n 441, February-March 1999, pp 114-115
•D McDowell, « Designers à Vallauris », *Résidences décoration*, July-August 1999, p VIII
•Karin Mecklenburg, « Design auf Rezept », *Architektur & Wohnen*, n 4, August-September 1999, p 16
•Enrico Morteo, « Dal mondo: i new designer e i nuovi prodotti, France, Ronan Bouroullec », *Interni*, n 492, July-August 1999, p 121
•*L'Œil*, July-August 1999, p 112
•Paquita Paquin, Cédric Saint-André Perrin, « Vous avez dit moderne? », supplement to *Libération*, 6 October 1999, pp 24-27
•Luisa Perlo, « Vallauris », *Artigianato*, n 34, August-September 1999, p 80
•« Profession designer: il redessine les meubles et les objets de la vie quotidienne », *Le Progrès de Cornouaille*, 29 August 1999, p 4
•Marco Romanelli, « Lo spirito del luogo », *Abitare*, n 382, March 1999, pp 160-165
•Marco Romanelli, « Dai saloni di Colonia Courtrai Parigi Londra, Un e demi, Erwan Bouroullec », *Abitare*, n 383, April 1999, p 199
•« Ronan Bouroullec », *Figaro Japan*, n 167, May 1999, p 153
•« Ronan Bouroullec at Harajuku Index », *Axis*, n 83, January-February 2000, p 117
•« Ronan Bouroullec: Hole Cappellini », *Abitare*, n 386, July-August 1999, p 61
•Anne-Cécile Sanchez, « Starckmania: la nouvelle garde du design », *Le Point*, 13 February 1999, pp 80-83
•Sophie de Santis, « Les combinaisons esthétiques de Ronan Bouroullec », *Figaroscope*, supplement to *Le Figaro*, 7 April 1999, p 5
•Sophie de Santis, « Diagnostic du confort bourgeois », *Numéro*, n 1, March 1999, p 36
•Virginie Seguin, « La Porcelaine dans tous ses états », *Résidences décoration*, 28, July-August 1999, p 32
•Danièle Semmel, « Ronan Bouroullec: ambivalent et anticonformiste », *Revue de l'ameublement*, 3, March 1999, pp 3-4
•David Souffan, « Ronan Bouroullec, un esprit singulier », *Résidences décoration*, 27, May-June 1999, pp 16-17
•Sophie Tasma Anargyro, « Ronan Bouroullec, les jeux de multiplication », *Intramuros*, n 82, April-May 1999, pp 36-41
•« Tasse all Folks », *Wallpaper**, 18, April 1999, p 272
•*Vacances bleues magazine*, n 18, 1999, p 9
•« Vallauris, céramiques contemporaines », *L'Humanité*, 3 August 1999
•« Vallauris invite les designers », *Intramuros*, June-July 1999
•Elisabeth Vedrenne, « Design: les épures de Ronan Bouroullec », *L'Œil*, n 509, September 1999, p 10
•Gareth Williams, « The New Vernacular », *Blueprint*, n 162, June 1999, p 28
•Edith Zapata, « L'Aventure du design », *Nice matin*, 7 April 1999
•Edith Zapata, « Picasso, Portanier et co... », *Nice matin*, 7 July 1999
•Edith Zapata, « Questions à Ronan Bouroullec et François Bauchet », *Nice matin*, 13 July 1999
•Maria Giulia Zunino, « News: Salon du Meuble de Paris », *Abitare*, n 390, December 1999, p 36

2000
Books
•Michel Bouisson, « L'utopie en œuvres, in *Design et utopies*, coll. « Les Villages », Industries Françaises de l'Ameublement / Hazan, Paris, 2000, pp 66, 68
•Mel Byars, *50 Beds, Innovations in Design and Materials*, coll. « Prodesign series », Crans-Près-Céligny, RotoVision, 2000, pp 44-47
•« Des cabanes », in *Babybloom*, (exh. cat.), 11-22 April 2000, Luisa delle Piane Gallery, Milan
•*La casa nel mondo*, Cappellini catalogue, cover and pp 16, 36, 53
•*Les Bons Génies de la vie domestique*, special issue *Beaux-Arts magazine*, Paris, 2000, pp 39, 43, 53, 57, 59
•*L'Objet design au quotidien*, (exh. cat.), 16 June-22 July 2000, Médiathèque Intercommunale de Miramas, p 9
•Brigitte Fitoussi, Giulio Cappellini, in *Design et utopies*, coll. « Les Villages », Industries Françaises de l'Ameublement / Hazan, Paris, 2000, p 23, 25
•Ingo Maurer, *The International Design Yearbook 2000*, London, Laurence King Publishing, 2000, pp 88, 138-139, 226
•Massimo Mutti, ed., « Ronan Bouroullec », in *Cappellini progetto oggetto*, Milan, 2000, np
•« Vases combinatoires, Ronan Bouroullec », in *Objets en mutation*, (exh. cat.), 24 November 2000-11 February 2001, Musée des Arts Décoratifs de Bordeaux, p 9
Articles
•Brice d'Antras, « Le Web et les designers », *Dizain*, n 24, Summer 2000, p 12
•Elisabeth Arkhipoff, « Le Design à la carte des frères Bouroullec », *Le Nouvel Observateur*, n 1877, 26 October 2000, pp 53-54
•Mireille Assénat, « Passez à l'orange », *Elle*, n 2862, 6 November 2000, p 265
•*Axis*, n 78, July-August 2000, p 122
•Jean-Luc Barberi, « Le XXIᵉ siècle s'annonce allongé », *L'Expansion*, n 626, 20 July 2000, p 115
•Thierry de Beaumont, « Giovani designer », *Interni*, n 500, April 2000, pp 12-13
•Mirko Beetschen, « Freiheit und Brüderlichkeit », *Ideales Heim*, das Schweizer Wohnmagazin, n 6, June 2000, pp 12-13
•Tonie Behar, « La Cuisine déconstruite de Ronan Bouroullec », *Citizen K international*, Spring 2000, p 32
•Lionel Blaisse, « Design contact, concepts industriels scénographiés », *Architecture intérieure CREE*, n 297, 2000, pp 58-61
•Julie Borgeaud, « Le Design italien se ressource avec des Français », *Paris Match*, n 2569, 11 May 2000, p 12
•Jean-Pierre Bourcier, « Objets balnéaires dans l'œil du design », *La Tribune*, 29 June 2000
•Fabrice Bousteau, « Christie's contemporain », special issue *Beaux-Arts magazine*, April 2000, np
•« Boutique A-POC », *Interni*, n 507, December 2000, p 192
•Ph C, « Design : archi-breton », *Le Nouvel Observateur*, n 3, February 2000, p 32
•Pascale Caussat, « Le Portfolio de Ronan Bouroullec », *Stratégies*, n 1142, 14 April 2000, p 44
•Michèle Champenois, « Le Quotidien en beauté, Ronan Bouroullec », supplement to *Le Monde*, « Beaubourg, d'un siècle à l'autre », p 11
•Alexandre P Charre, « 100% design », *It magazine*, n 2, November-December 2000, p 135
•Jérôme Coignard, « Plastique art », *AD, Les plus belles maisons du monde*, n 7, November 2000, pp 100-105
•Lauretta Coz, « Fratelli Bouroullec », *Casamica*, n 6, 14 June 2000, pp 98-103
•Julie Crysler, « French Kiss », *Azure, Design Architecture and Art*, May-June 2000, pp 88-89
•« Design, design à Hyères », *Var matin*, 30 June 2000
•« Design : ils savent arrondir les angles », *Paris Match*, 2658, 4 May 2000, p 118
•« Design : lancez-vous dans le confort plex », *Paris Match*, n 2533, 3 February 2000, pp 94-98
•« Design-moi la villa Noailles », *Beaux-Arts magazine*, August 2000
•« Designers White Legs », *Financial Times Weekend*, 15 April 2000, pp 29-32
•Sophie Djerlal, « Con un Salon du meuble... », *Vogue Italia*, January 2000
•Sophie Djerlal, « Design: il rendez-vous è a Parigi... », *Vogue Italia*, January 2000
•Bénédicte Duhalde, « Périmètres en liberté », *Intramuros*, n 87, February-March 2000, p 47
•« Erwan Bouroullec: Lit Clos, One and a Half Sofa », *Design*, April 2000, p 245
•« Expanding House, Ronan Bouroullec per Interni », *Interni*, n 497, January-February 2000, pp 96-97
•Claire Fayolle, « Ces lumineux objets du design », *Beaux-Arts magazine*, 199, December 2000, pp 86-89
•Anne-Marie Fèvre, « Du cœur à l'ouvrage », *Libération*, n 5958, 13 July 2000, p 39
•Anne-Marie Fèvre, « Designers horspistes », *Libération*, 4 February 2000
•Anne-Marie Fèvre, « Fenêtres sur Hyères », dossier « Un été 2000 », *Libération*, n 5976, 3 August 2000, p IV
•Brigitte Fitoussi, « Un nouvel esprit boutique, Ronan Bouroullec », interview, d'A *D'Architectures*, n 6, November 2000, pp 32-33
•Brigitte Fitoussi, « Paris janvier 2000, Il Salone del Mobile di Parigi », *Design Diffusion News*, n 77, March 2000, pp 178-182
•Brigitte Fitoussi, « Paris janvier 2000, Esposizione "Byob" alla galleria Neotu », *Design Diffusion News*, n 77, March 2000, pp 200-201
•Brigitte Fitoussi , « Plage à la page », *Numéro*, 15, August 2000, p 34
•« Focus », interview, *Monitor Unlimited*, n 6, 2000, pp 60-69
•Christiane Germain, « AD rencontres », *AD, Les plus belles maisons du monde*, n 4, July-August 2000, pp 14-15
•Christiane Germain, « Les Frères Ronan et Erwan Bouroullec, designers : l'élégance intérieure », *Télérama*, n 2622, 15 April 2000, p 62
•Nathalie Giraud, « Plages de luxe », *Madame Figaro*, 19 August 2000
•Serge Gleizes, « Design à géométrie variable », *Table et cadeau, l'objet pour la maison et l'hôtellerie*, n 422, December 1999-January 2000, pp 52-53
•Shinita Groinch, « Table rase », *Jalouse*, n 35, November 2000, p 38
•Chantale Hamaide, « Hyères design », *Intramuros*, July 2000
•Chantale Hamaide, « Design Attitude », *Intramuros*, n 90, August-September 2000, p 72
•Chantale Hamaide, « Le Design installe un rendez-vous d'été », *Intramuros*, n 90, August-September 2000, pp 30-32
•Chantale Hamaide, « L'Éclosion de la chrysalide », *Intramuros*, n 90, August-September 2000, p 42
•Martine Henno, « Styles de vie, je concepte, tu conceptes, il concepte... Issey Miyake », *Le Figaro*, n 17450, 18 September 2000, p 20
•« Huis clos », *Ateliers d'Art*, n 26, March-April 2000, p 8
•Nikola Jankovic, « 2001 Le Design, entretien avec les Bouroullec », *Crash*, n 15, December 2000-January 2001, pp 60-63
•Françoise Jaunin, « Radi et les Bouroullec à l'Ecal, les étoiles de

l'après Starck », *24 heures, sport, culture, société*, 29 March 2000, p 40
•Sophie Lemoine, « Issey Miyake: A-POC, c'est impec! », *Sites Archi*, n 102, October-November 2000, pp 6-7
•Jean-Yves Manac'h, « Les grands noms de la création les réclament aux quatre coins du monde, Les Bouroullec: designers quimpérois », *Ouest France*, n 17079, 28 December 2000, p 7
•« Metropole, Ronan et Erwan Bouroullec », *Axis*, n 84, March-April 2000, p 98
•Cristina Morozzi, « Dall'ordinario allo straordinario », *Interni*, n 504, September 2000, p 225
•Birgit Müller, « Showdown in Mailand », *Design Report*, July-August 2000, pp 43-54
•« OFF ICCF », *Interni*, n 503, July-August 2000, p 18
•Paquita Paquin, « Quelle A-POC », *Libération*, n 6009, 11 September 2000, p 41
•Paquita Paquin, C Saint André Perrin, « Tendances d'Hyères », *Libération*, 28 April 2000, p 45
•Laurence Picot, « Sous le signe des Bouroullec », *Ideat*, n 7, July-August 2000, pp 20-21
•Henri Plouïdy, « Trente étudiants réinventent la roue », *Habiter, le temps immobilier*, supplement to *Le Temps*, n 12, 3 April 2000, pp 4-5
•Eva Praquin, « À pas feutrés », *Résidences Décoration*, n 31, March-April 2000, p 88
•« Quelle maison pour demain? », *Courrier du meuble et de l'habitat*, n 7 January 2000
•Alice Rawsthorn, « Maximal Minimalist », *I.D. The International Design Magazine*, n 40, January-February 2000, pp 3, 108-109
•Alice Rawsthorn, « Object Lesson », *Financial Times Weekend*, 22-23 July 2000, p 10
•Pascale Renaux, « Panorama, nouveaux endroits, pourquoi on y va? », *Numéro*, n 17, October 2000, p 108
•« Rendez-vous à Hyères », *Stratégies*, 18 July 2000
•Marco Romanelli, « Pezzi singoli: Erwan Bouroullec », *Abitare*, n 397, July-August 2000, p 154
•Laurence Salmon, « Le design s'expose dans les galeries », *Dizain*, n 24, Summer 2000, p 30
•Sanchez, Anne-Cécile, « Design, les frères touche-à-tout », *Le Point*, n 1460, 8 September 2000, p. 50
•Sophie de Santis, « Erwan Bouroullec, l'intimité suspendue », *Figaroscope*, supplement to *Le Figaro*, 9 February 2000
•Christian Simenc, « Objets dernier cri », *Marie-Claire Maison*, n 361, November 2000, pp 38-39
•« Special Feature », *Nikkei Design*, January 2000, p 43
•Julie Street, « Life after Starck », *Where Paris*, n 77, May 2000, pp 12-13
•Caroline Tiné, « Visions du IIIᵉ millénaire: les designers attaquent, Ronan et Erwan Bouroullec », *Marie-Claire*

Maison, n 354, December 1999-January 2000, pp 16-17
•« Un air de vacances », *L'Usine nouvelle*, 22 June 2000
•Laure Verchère, « L'œil aux aguets de Pierre Staudenmeyer: la Galerie Neotu », *Elle Décoration*, n 97, May 2000, p 45
•Marion Vignal, « Construit moi une cabane », *L'Express*, n 2563, 17 August 2000, p 15
•Marion Vignal, « Le design balnéaire », *L'Express*, n 2564, 24 August 2000
•« Villa Noailles, le design d'Erwan Bouroullec », *Maison française*, July 2000
•« Vive la Bretagne », *Maison française*, n 505, April-May 2000, p 19
•Dominique Wagner, « Design 2000, les frères Bouroullec », *AMC*, n 109, September 2000, p 30
•Geneviève Welcomme, « Les frères Bouroullec à la villa Noailles », *La Croix*, n 35668, 15-16 July 2000, p 15

2001

Books
•*Ambiance Magasin* [exh. cat.], Abbaye Saint-André, Centre d'Art Contemporain, Meymac, 2001, np
•E Company, B Dard, « Le Pichet, le seau à glaçons, le bac à glace de Ronan et Erwan Bouroullec », in *Design Dezinc*, [exb. cat.], 24 April-25 May 2001, Espace Paul Ricard, np
•Anne-Marie Fèvre, « R & E Bouroullec », *Beaux-Arts Magazine*, special issue 4: « Le design, objets, tendances, styles », 2001, pp 130-131
•Charlotte and Peter Fiell, « R. & E. Bouroullec », *Designing the 21ˢᵗ century*, Taschen, Cologne, 2001, p. 88-93
•Catherine Geel, « Ronan et Erwan Bouroullec » and « Domeau & Pérès », in *Design et gammes*, coll. « Les Villages », Industries Françaises de l'Ameublement / Hazan, Paris, 2001, pp 136-137 and 144
•*Manger/Eat*, n 2, Coromandel Design, Paris, 2001, pp 222-227
•« Ronan Bouroullec », in *Art contemporain : un choix de deux cents œuvres du Fonds national d'art contemporain (1985-1999)*, éditions du Chêne, Paris, 2001, p. 68
•« Ronan & Erwan Bouroullec: Glide; Tavolo & Tavolino; Brick », *Zoo*, n 10, September 2001, p 117
•Laurence Salmon, *Ronan & Erwan Bouroullec* [exh. cat.], 31 May-28 July 2001, Kreo Gallery, Paris
•Laurence Salmon, *Ronan & Erwan Bouroullec* [exh. cat.], 24 November-22 December 2001, Miyake Design Studio, Tokyo
Articles
•Marjorie Alessandrini, « Design: dans un fauteuil », *Le Nouvel Observateur*, 13 September 2001, p 44
•« A-POC », *Monitor Unlimited*, n 2, 2001, pp 90-93
•« A-POC, Erwan & Ronan Bouroullec », *Casa Brutus*, n 13, April 2001, p 38
•« Architecture commerciale »,

Archinews, l'actualité sensible, March 2001, pp 52-55
•S Astier, T Billard, J M Dubois, M Mine, « Paris, capitale du design, Ronan et Erwan Bouroullec: le sens de l'utile », *Paris Capitale*, n 68, March 2001, p 43
•Laurence Benaïm, « Hommes, la mode en capital », supplement to *Le Monde*, 25 September 2001, pp I, VIII
•Violaine Binet, « French Touch, la nouvelle vague », *Vogue Paris*, n 814, February 2001, pp 251-255
•Myriam Boutoulle, « Von der Rolle », *Design Report*, January 2001, p 10
•Myriam Boutoulle, « Au quotidien, Coromandel express », *Connaissance des Arts*, n 584, June 2001, p 128
•Laurence Boyer, « Rituel ludique, Boutiques Mandarina Duck et Issey Miyake, R et E Bouroullec, designers », *Techniques & Architecture*, n 451, December 2000-January 2001, pp 126-127
•« Cappellini, il punto di incontro del design internazionale », *Corriere della Sera*, n 4, April 2001, p 2
•Véronique Cauhapé, « La Maison du futur recherche respiration », *Le Monde*, n 17409, 13 January 2001, p 25
•Michèle Champenois, « La Villa Noailles, rendez-vous estival de jeunes designers », *Le Monde*, 12 August 2001
•Alexandre Charre, « Vers de nouveaux modèles d'habitation », *It magazine*, n 3, 2001, pp 120-121
•Lauretta Coz, « Parlano i giovani creativi stranieri », *Corriere della Sera*, 4 April 2001, p 3
•« Design Paris 4ᵉ : A-POC, vêtements à transformations », *Intramuros*, special issue, 2002, p 38
•Pierre Doze, « Aux classes laborieuses », *Intramuros*, n 94, April-May 2001, p 40
•Armand Dulac, « De l'école à l'objet », *Ikea Room*, n 4, Winter 2001, p 32
•I Dupont, L Picot, « Tendance: black is back », *Paris Match*, 18 October 2001, p 22
•Tom Dyckhoff, « Nouveau riche », *The Guardian Space*, 5 April 2001, pp 10-11
•Ph Ellen, « Design: Bouroullec brothers », *Tribeca*, n 2, Summer 2001, p 30
•« Evisu project: Ronan & Erwan Bouroullec », *Casa Vogue*, n 9, October 2001, p 43
•Giusi Ferrè, « A-POC, l'invention de la pièce unique », *Cartier magazine*, n 1, Autumn 2001, pp 48-53
•Anne-Marie Fèvre, « Tendance design, la ligne claire », *Libération*, 13 January 2001, pp 46-47
•Anne-Marie Fèvre, « La Combinaison Bouroullec », *Libération*, 26 June 2001, p 33
•Sigrid von Fischern, « Adieu chichibonJour Jeunesse: Ronan und Erwan Bouroullec », *Design Report*, January 2001, pp 54-55
•Brigitte Fitoussi, « Milan 2001 », *Numéro*, n 24, June 2001, pp 38-41
•Brigitte Fitoussi, « Le Design français fait flamber la côte », *Série Limitée*, n 9, pp 40-42

•Brigitte Fitoussi, Christophe Pillet, « Giulio Cappellini », *Repères 01*, Salon du Meuble de Paris 2001, 11-15 January 2001, np
•Chantal Hamaide, « La vitrine du design à Manhattan », *Intramuros*, n 96, August-September 2001, pp 64-76
•Chantal Hamaide, « A-POC, vêtements à transformation », *Intramuros*, special issue « Design Paris », 2001, p 34
•Chantal Hamaide, Pierre Doze, « Rive droite/rive gauche, design italien et équilibre parisien », *Intramuros*, n 96, August-September 2001, pp 58-61
•Masae Hara, « The Artistic Party by Colette », *La Vie de 30 ans*, n 4, April 2001, p 33
•Esther Henwood, « Envie de… », *Architecture Digest*, n 13, June 2001, p 28
•« In nome del Corian® », *Case da abitare*, n 46, April 2001, p 56
•Julie Iovine, « In Milan, Form Follows Fashion », *The New York Times*, 12 April 2001
•Laurent Jacques, « Erwan et Ronan Bouroullec, les frères magiques », *Univers magazine*, n 6, March-April 2001, pp 60-62
•*M K, Interior Design Magazine*, n 6, 2001, p 28
•Meyer von Klaus, « Bunter Luxus-teurer Pop », *Design Report*, July-August 2001, pp 30-38
•Sophie Lemoine, « La Galère des jeunes créateurs », *Le Figaro*, 2 February 2001, p 16
•Sophie Lemoine, « Ronan et Erwan Bouroullec, 29 et 25 ans, designers », *USD*, n 1219, 4 January 2001, p 28
•« Les vingt personnalités de la nouvelle génération », special issue « Paris is Burning », *Barfout!* pp 16, 31
•Laura Maggi, « Progetti di famiglia », *Elle Decor*, April 2001, pp 45-48
•Françoise Mainguet, « Les frères Bouroullec », interview, *It magazine*, n 2, pp 76-77
•Irene Meier, « Avangardisten der Jungen Garde », *Raum und Wohnen*, October-November 2001, pp 194-199
•Suzy Menkes, « Miyake's Slice-Your-Own », *Herald Tribune*, 4 September 2001
•Cristina Morozzi, « Issey Miyake: la forma di un'idea », *Interni*, n 508, January-February 2001, pp 126-131
•Judit Osvart, « Young Titans, Ronan and Erwan Bouroullec », *Atrium*, February-March 2001, pp 74-75
•R P, « G-Mark-Verleihung : Issey Miyake Erhält für A-Poc Japans Höchsten Design Preis », *Form*, n 178, March-April 2001, p 94
•« Passion for fashion », *Uhmepbep*, n 9, pp 59-61
•Francesca Picchi, « The Infinite Shades of Meaning », *Domus*, n 840, September 2001, pp 122-129
•Mia Pizzi, « 5 x 2, Cappellini », *Case da abitare*, January-February 2001, p 190
•José Postic, « Un design bien assis », *Marie-Claire Maison*, n 365, May-June 2001, p 209
•Jean Bond Rafferty, « Discovering design », *France Magazine*, Summer

2001, pp 16-31
• Alice Rawsthorn, « Frère Deal », *Harper's Bazaar*, March 2001, pp 323-324
• Alice Rawsthorn, « Life: Frères deal », *Harper's Bazaar*, June 2001, pp 169-170
• Fabienne Reybaud, « Les Deux Frères », *DS Magazine*, n 45, February 2001, pp 142-143
• Marco Romanelli, « A-POC/Miyake », *Abitare*, n 402, January 2001, pp 78-79
• Marco Romanelli, « Salone 2001: Cappellini », *Abitare*, n 409, September 2001, pp 116-117
• Marco Romanelli, « Microambiente », *Abitare*, n 411, November 2001, p 195
• « Ronan & Erwan Bouroullec », *Axis*, n 90, March-April 2001, p 37
• « Ronan et Erwan Bouroullec », *Designers' Workshop*, n 117, August 2001, p 58
• Felicia du Rouret, « Un design convivial », *Maison Madame Figaro*, n 23, December 2001, pp 134-135
• Caroline Roux, « Designer Living: the Bouroullec Brothers », *The Guardian Space*, 5 April 2001, p 34
• Zoë Ryan, « Cappellini, Shelflife », *Surface*, n 30, p 70
• Chris Scott, « Soft Machine », *Frame*, n 18, January-February 2001, pp 76-83
• Yann Siliec, « Pas de 2 », *UpStreet*, n 29, June 2001, pp 54-57
• Francesca Taroni, « Luce senza confini », *Case da abitare*, n 52, November 2001, pp 57-62
• Marion Vignal, « Les frères Bouroullec en toute simplicité », *L'Express le Magazine*, n 2006, 3 May 2001, pp 22-24
• Agnes Waendendries, « AD talents: Vallauris, des céramiques utilitaires », *Architecture Digest*, n 13, June 2001, pp 166-167
• Miranda Westwood, « French profile », *FX*, September 2001, pp 60-66
• Sarah Wright, «Très chic », *The Guardian Space*, 5 April 2001, pp 18-19
• Eric Wuilmot, « Dé-placer…», *Architectures à Vivre*, n 6, Winter 2001, pp 16-19, 21

2002
Books
• Nathalie Chapuis, ed., *Créateurs, Création en France: la scène contemporaine*, Autrement / CNDP, Paris, 2002, pp 28-34, 220-225
• Laurent Le Bon, *Ronan et Erwan Bouroullec: catalogue de raison*, Images Modernes / Kreo, Paris, 2002
• « Ronan et Erwan Bouroullec », in *Design & etalages*, coll. « Design & », Industries Françaises de l'Ameublement / Le Seuil, Paris, 2002, pp 130-131
• « Ronan + Erwan Bouroullec », in *Spoon*, London, Phaidon, 2002, pp 92-95
Articles
• « Actualités, produits », *Intramuros*, n 98, December 2001-January 2002, pp 80, 104
• Yoko Amakawa « Ronan and Erwan Bouroullec in MDS/G », *Living Design*, n 22, March-April 2002, pp 84-87

• « A-POC », *Intramuros*, special issue, 2002, p 38
• J B, « Cabanes design », *Vogue Paris*, n 826, April 2002, p 79
• Emma BaJac, « Ma cabane à Hyères », *DizaJn*, n 31, Spring 2002, p 15
• Tonie Behar, « Fraternellement vôtre », *Edgar*, n 13, September-October 2002, pp 108-111
• Anna Bernagozzi, « Brotherly Love », *Design Week*, 31 January 2002, pp 22-26
• Martin Béthenod, « Fraternité », *Vogue Paris*, n 833, December 2002-January 2003, pp 164-165
• « Bouroullec, la famille design », *Rézo International*, n 8, Spring-Summer 2002, pp 26-27
• Marie-France Boyer, « The Bouroullec Brothers », *The World of Interiors*, February 2002, pp 89-94
• Alessandra Burigana, « Ronan e Erwan Bouroullec: l'essenzialismo », *Casamica*, April 2002, pp 197-201
• Catherine Croft, « Brotherly Love », *Building Design*, 28 March 2002, pp 16-17
• Wojciech Czaja, « What's Cooking? », *H.O.M.E.*, February 2002, pp 98-101
• Simon Das, « Brother Beyond », *I. D. The International Design Magazine*, n 219, April 2002, p 58
• Henri-François Debailleux, « Un marché couvert à tous les genres », *Libération*, 22 January 2002, p 34
• Pierre Doze, « Milan 2002: Less + More, et d'autres choses encore », *Intramuros*, n 101, June-July 2002, p 70
• Tom Dyckhoff, « A French Revolution », *The Guardian Weekend Magazine*, 19 January 2002
• M E, « Et Krzentowski créa Kréo », *Un, deux… quatre arts & cultures*, n 206, April-June 2002, pp 21-23
• Brigitte Fitoussi, « Duo de choc », *Numéro*, n 32, April 2002, pp 66-68
• Caroline Goossens, « Frans & Fris: The Fabulous Bouroullec Boys », *Items*, n 4, September-October 2002, pp 68-69
• Hens von Gregor, « Das Wohnzimmer von Erwan und Ronan Bouroullec », *Süddeutsche Zeitung*, 4 April 2002, pp 8-14
• Sarah de Haro, « Agenda: un été à la villa Noailles », *Mixte*, n 18, April-May 2002, pp 44-45
• « The Heirs Apparent », *Metro London*, 25 January 2002
• Mark Hooper, « Sit-up, Straight-up: Erwan and Ronan Bouroullec », *I.D. The International Design Magazine*, n 219, April 2002, p 50
• Jednolita Kresba, « Ronan a Erwan Bouroullecovi », *Blok*, January 2002, pp 32-37
• Emmanuelle Lequeux, « Design: cibler la sensation plutôt que la fonction », *Aden*, supplement to *Le Monde*, 13-19 February 2002, p 25
• Dominic Lutyens, « French Ticklers », *Design Profile*, January 2002
• Dominic Lutyens, « Vive la France », *The Observer*, 27 January 2002, pp 88-89
• «Made in France: Ronan et Erwan Bouroullec », *Experimenta*, n 40, May

2002, pp 112-113
• Yukari Miyamoto, « L'eau d'Issey-Three New Forms », *Axis*, n 97, May-June 2002, pp 76-80
• Elisa Morère, « Hedi Slimane face à Ronan Bouroullec », *Le Figaro*, 25-26 May 2002, p 18
• Mathias Ohrel, « Industrie légère », *Les Inrockuptibles*, n 333, 10-16 April 2002, pp 84-85
• Lars Hedebo Olsen, « Design til Nomader », *Berlingske Tidende*, 23 June 2002, cover and p 4
• Judit Osvart, « Pillango airbrushsal: interjù Ronan Bouroullec », *Atrium*, June-July 2002, pp 68-71
• Marcella Ottolenghi, « Una certa positiva leggerezza », *Box*, n 25, January 2002, pp 122-124
• Rachael Philipps, « French Fancy », *Time Out*, January-February 2002, p 31
• Francesca Picchi, « Lavorare al bar, Working at the Bar », *Domus*, n 853, November 2002, pp 110-117
• Francesca Picchi, Maria Cristina Tommasini, « Design morbido: Soft Design », *Domus*, n 848, May 2002, p 122
• Laurence Picot, « Les Bouroullec: la fraternité du design », *Elle Décoration*, n 116, April 2002, pp 81-84
• « Questions à cent designers », *Intramuros*, special issue, n 100, April-May 2002, pp 58, 94, 152
• Ragey-Gracé, « La Petite maison dans le jardin de la villa Noailles », *Connaissance des Arts*, n 593, April 2002, p 26
• Manuela Ravasio, « Erwan & Ronan Bouroullec. Se il tappeto diventa un monolocale… », *Gulliver*, n 4, April 2002, pp 196, 198
• Catherine Rigollet, « Bouroullec, frères design », *Magazine Air France*, n 60, April 2002, p 153
• « Ronan & Erwan Bouroullec », *Pen*, n 83, 2002, p 50
• Schönwetter, « Zurück in die Zukunft », *Design Report*, November 2002, pp 34-36
• « Talent Spotting: the Bouroullec Boys », *Elle Deco*, February 2002, pp 35-36
• « Watch me!: Ronan & Erwan Bouroullec », *Title*, July 2002, p 35
• Andrea Weisbrod, « Erwan et Ronan Bouroullec », *H.O.M.E.*, January-February 2002, p 87

2003
Articles
• Lucia Allais, « Joyn: les frères Bouroullec », *Workspirit*, n 8, pp 4-11
• Anne-Marie Fèvre, « En moins de deux », *Libération*, 14 January 2003
• François Gaillard, « Ronan et Erwan Bouroullec », *Architecture Intérieure CREE*, n 307, February-March 2003, pp 98-99
• Anna Lombardi, « Ambiente su misura », *Ottagono*, n 157, February 2003, pp 114-117
• Mark Rappolt, « Artist Project : The Brothers Bouroullec », *Tate International Arts and Culture*,

March-April 2003, pp 64-72
• Marco Romanelli, « Clouds », *Abitare*, n 426, March 2003, pp 164-165
• Christian Simenc, « Ronan et Erwan Bouroullec, designers Frères de sens », *Le Journal des arts*, n 162, pp 13-15
• Stephen Todd, « O Brothers, Where Art Thou? », *Men's Fashion of the Times, New York Times Magazine*, n 9 March 2003

Photographic Credits

Ronan and Erwan Bouroullec: p 7,
p 8 right, n 6, n 47-48, n 58-59,
n 61-62, n 65, n 73-74, p 86
centre right, right, n 105-106,
n 112, n 116, n 120-121, p 114-115,
n 152-156, n 161, n 164, n 172,
n 176, n 179-181, n 189-190
Geoffrey Cottenceau and Julien
Gaillardot : all the photographic
compositions
Marc Domage: n 122
Dominique Freintrenie: n 1, n 7
Fulguro: n 5
Neotu Gallery: n 177
Rendel & Spitz Gallery:
n 208 -212
Morgane Le Gall: p 8 centre,
n 2-3, n 8, p 18 left, centre,
n 10-14, n 18, p 58 right, n 76-86,
n 88-91, n 97, p 86 centre, n 113,
n 117-118, n 128-129, p 124 left,
right, n 137-142, n 148, n 160,
p 148 left, centre left, n 163,
n 165, n 169-171, p 170 centre
left, centre back, right, n 186,
n 188, n 191, n 194
Paul Tahon : p 8 left, n 9, p 18
right, p 28-29 centre, n 19,
n 22-30, n 32, n 92-95, n 97,
n 99-103, n 109-111, n 114-115,
n 119, n 126-127, p 116 left,
centre, n 132-136, p 148 centre,
centre right, right, n 162 ,
n 166-168, n 175, n 178, n 184-185,
p 170 left, centre front, centre
right, n 192-193, n 195-197,
n 199-200, p 183, p 192 left, right,
n 204, n 206, n 208, n 213,
n 215-216
Miro Zagnoli : p 42 left, right,
n 63-64, n 69-72, n 75

Credits

The publisher would like to thank
Ronan and Erwan Bouroullec
along with all the contributing
authors, including Claude Aïello,
Lucia Allais, Andrea Branzi, Giulio
Cappellini, Rolf Fehlbaum, Issey
Miyake and David Toppani.
Many thanks to Morgane Le Gall,
Cappellini, Geoffrey Cottenceau,
Julien Gaillardot and the École
Cantonale d'Art de Lausanne,
Marc Domage, Dominique
Feintrenie, Fulguro, Kreo Gallery,
Neotu Gallery, Rendel & Spitz
Gallery, Paul Tahon, Vitra and
Miro Zagnoli for providing images.
Thanks are also due to Perrine
Vigneron and Marie Compagnon
for their valuable help

To learn more about Phaidon, to keep up to date with our publications, to
sign up to our newsletter, and to benefit from special promotions, visit us at
www.phaidon.com